I0541983

Copyright © 2024 Freedom Boy Publishing LLC

All rights reserved. No part of this book may be reproduced or used in any manner without the prior written permission of the copyright owner, except for the use of brief quotations in a book review.

To request permissions, contact the author at arash@arashjacob.com

Paperback ISBN: 979-8-218-32495-7

Cover and book design by Jason Arias

Printed in the United States of America

Freedom Boy

The Power of One Child's Inner Wisdom

Arash Jacob

A Memoir

Dedication

To Mr. McDonald, my 9th Grade English teacher, for reading
my summer essay out loud to the whole class, and for saying that
it made the hair on the back of your neck stand straight up!
Thank you for reflecting my work back to me.

To Mr. Mills-Coyne, my 10th Grade English teacher, for allowing
the deep love between us to show in your forever smile, for using
my question as a prompt the very next day, and for posting my papers
on the wall, nearly universally stamped "First Class." Your love is the
foundation of support upon which this book is written.

To both of you: You inspire me still and stand priceless in my heart.
I have no words to thank you.

For English teachers everywhere.

Contents

Introduction

My parents divorced when I was four. Then, a sudden change to the country's leadership made everyone choose: Leave quickly or be jailed, have your home seized, and if deemed against the new regime, be killed.

Many took off in a big hurry. My father hated his mother, and so punished mine by taking us away from Mom before she could get her paperwork together to leave. What my mother experienced from having her children stripped away from her and left in the country is impossible for me to imagine, still.

My father, sister, and I rolled through Switzerland, their cobblestoned streets and high-tower brothels; White Plains, New York, long enough to remember school; Maryland for a summer; then landed in Florida, where our story begins.

Even though the first few years were a heart-breaking mess, Florida life somehow had a magical thread through it. All was not lost.

I remember walking through my neighborhood there, at seven years old, feeling there was something else in this world that no one was explaining. I felt it between the cars and the trees and the mounds of construction dirt we played on—between all the physical reality I could see. I knew there was something else in this world, and I knew that it knew I was there.

This relationship with the unseen grabbed my life and navigated it. Well, I didn't realize it was the unseen until I was about thirty.

I never intended to write a book. I never thought I would. Looking back, I used to love to come up with titles, and the beginnings of stories seemed to pop up everywhere. Early in high school English classes, I'd begin writing my essays due that day on the morning bus ride to school. At lunch, I'd write the second draft in the library—like in a speedy rush, and hand it in right after, in fifth period. Somehow, I nearly always received high praise for the hurried work. Apparently, life was bent on squeezing my love out of me, despite my monstrous protest against it.

At thirty-five years old, I heard a voice, seemingly out of the blue: "You must write," it said.

By that point, I knew enough to listen to that kind of voice, but I didn't know what to write. *Write,* I thought. What the heck am I supposed to write? I didn't know what to write, so I started writing poetry. Mom wrote poetry, so I wrote. I wrote a lot. After trying halfheartedly to get some published, I lost steam and set it aside.

Two years later, while spring cleaning, I came across it in a drawer. I picked up the thick stack in both hands, looked at the top page, sat for a moment, and had a flash: It's all my mother's pain. I calmly walked to the garbage can, gently placed the stack inside, and turned and walked away. A hundred pounds lifted off my shoulders.

But the words, "You must write," kept coming. I kept hearing them every day. The same message. The same tone—consistent and strong.

I then fumbled around, writing stories about my life, and deleted two second-draft books, until one day, the vision for this book appeared. Suddenly, I knew the beginning and the end. And I knew I just had to fill in the middle.

For the next four years, I dragged my feet through fear, anxiety, inspiration, procrastination, and the love of writing. The fear of facing my own story, my own self, would paralyze me for hours, sometimes days. But I'd return again.

They say that the memoir is the easiest book to publish but the hardest to write. I raise my right hand and attest to the hardest-to-write part, yes sir.

I deeply hope that my labor of love and countless hours of smiles, spontaneous elations, and fist pull-downs at my side while shouting, "Yes!" as a sentence or idea came into perfection touches you as it does me, and that bringing you by my side inspires you as it does me.

CHAPTER ONE

Science Shock

"Okay, class, turn to page 121 in your books. Today we are going to study *centripetal force*. This is going to be cool."

That sounds cool. I flip through my book quickly, then slowly as I get close to the page. Ah, page 121! I look at Mr. Crock and sit soldier straight.

"Hey, Arash, you really like science, huh?" James looks at me, still flipping.

"Yeah, it's pretty cool. And Mr. Crock is great."

"Right. He likes you a lot. That's awesome. And he is pretty cool."

"Now, centripetal force is the inward gravitational force that our earth exerts on our moon. The earth's gravity pulls you to the center of it. Similarly, the earth's gravity tugs on the moon, keeping it close. Gravity, therefore, works like a string, tugging on the moon. Cut the string and release the gravity, and the moon flies away. We call the inward force of that gravity centripetal force. It's always inward."

"Psst, James. So clear, so easy, how can you not love this guy? Does anybody explain stuff better?"

James looks at me like I'm nuts.

"All right, class, who can—"

Click, click. The class door opens, Dad sticks his head in, and the rest of him comes in too. He's breathing heavy.

"Uh, yes, teacher, sir." Dad raises his hand to Mr. Crock. "May I speak with you? It is an urgent matter."

Mr. Crock waves him close.

Dad rushes nervously and talks in a low voice.

"Arash, grab your things and come to the front, please." Mr. Crock waves me over calmly. "Arash, your father has a release from the principal. It looks like you'll be leaving us for a short while, son. We'll miss you." He smiles at me, like a hundred hugs landing and squeezing me tight. "It's been a joy having you in my class, that's for sure." He smiles more, deep, like he's known me forever.

I want to smile, but I don't know what to do.

"Uh, professor, sir. I do apologize again about this, but it is urgent, and we are sorry for disturbing class. Arash does like his teachers very much and he does work very hard. We do appreciate everything you and all his teachers do for him." Dad takes a teeny step back. He's itching to leave.

Mr. Crock's eyes shine bright at both of us, and he motions to Dad. "He's one of my best." He turns to me like we're equals.

I smile. "Thank you, Mr. Crock."

"Here you are, Mr. Jacob," Mr. Crock says, handing Dad back his release slip.

Dad takes it and puts his arm around me, and we head out the door. As soon as we're out, he starts jogging. "Come on, man! Let's get to the car. I'll explain there. Come!"

I jog behind him. "What's going on?"

"Get inside the car. Come on, let's go!"

Just as we get in and close the doors, he slams it into drive, and we tear out of school and down the street. "Shit, man! Fuck!" He smashes the steering wheel with both hands and slams the brakes, jerking us forward at the stop sign.

"What's going on?" I turn to him in my seat.

The back of his hand rubs the sweat off his upper lip, and then he wipes his face. "Listen, man—some shit went down." He looks right and left, then takes off like a maniac. "Fuck, man. I fucked up! Some shit went down with Shelby and me, and she got so fuckin' pissed. Fuck! Then she went crazy, man. She said she was going to call Child Protective Services and tell them I've been sleeping in a different house and that I was leaving a twelve-year-old alone at night. She said they would come and take you from me. Fuck that shit. I ain't letting nobody take you anywhere."

I look around the car, in it, and outside. "What?"

"Yeah, man. You know we were arguing pretty bad. That shit got hot. You know, fuck her. Maybe she said that shit to hurt me, but I am not taking no chances. She had that look in her eye, man—she was fuckin' serious. And I knew if she got pissed enough, she would do it, too. We're going to the Army Navy now. We get you a duffle bag and you go to California and stay with your mother and your sister until this shit cools down. Then I bring you back. I bring you back, no problems, for sure, man. Not to worry."

My brain explodes.

"Army Navy Surplus," the huge sign that I've seen a million times reads. Except today, I don't like that it's here. I don't like that I'm here. I don't like anything about any of this.

We jump out and jog inside. Down the backpack aisle, at the very end, Dad kneels and starts pulling duffle bags off the bottom shelf like a machine gun, throwing most of them behind him in a crazy mess.

"What size, Pop?"

"Extra extra large. Look only for XXL."

"Got it!" I hand him one.

He tears the plastic off and pulls the straps from the seams as hard as he can, trying to tear them. It's the same thing he does on my backpacks every year to make sure the stitching isn't junk. "Good." He scoops up all the bags on the floor and throws them on the shelf, just for them to slide back down as we jog away.

* * *

After a couple of stoplights, I turn back to see the duffle in the back seat. The cotton is so thick–tank-like–with double and triple stitching everywhere. I sit back. Suddenly my head is like broken glass floating in slow motion around me. Going to California? Staying with Mom? What?

"Listen, man, we gotta get home now. We put all your clothes and everything you need into the duffle bag. We pack it nice and good, and then we get you on a plane. You know, I'm sorry to have to rush, but we have to move–there is no time."

My eyes are heavy. I want to sleep, but he keeps swerving. My head starts to fall. We hit a bump, and I snap awake. Dad wipes his eyes with the back of his hand. He's crying, and my chest gets achy. Don't cry now, Arash. He'll be even more sad. Help him. Say something to him. The air between us gets quiet, and it's like I'm so far away. The trees and stores along the road are moving so fast, but everything in this car is like moving in mud.

We park, bust out, and race into our room.

"Go to your dresser drawers, Son. Toss me the clothes, and I will shove it in." He lays the duffle out long and flat on the floor and opens the mouth end, into which, like a sausage, we're supposed to pack my whole life. I toss clothes. Dad catches and shovels. I empty the entire dresser and the bag is only a third full. I go to the closet.

"Good job, Son. Keep it coming."

I do.

"Arash, now take my toiletry bag and put your toothpaste, toothbrush, and counter things in there and let's get those."

We look around and then at each other.

His soft and sad eyes are so hard to look at.

"Let's go now to the pool hall."

"Pool hall?"

"Yeah. We have about an hour and a half to kill before we go to the airport. Come on. Let's go."

We're back in the car, and my elbow rests on the car door—half in, half out, and the warm wind blowing on me isn't nearly as awesome as it usually is. California? Wonder how Mom is over there? What is she like now? Happy? We cruise up our street, cross 441, and head into a strip mall. Off to the right, my eye catches a little Irish bar I never noticed.

"We going there?" I point. "Larry's Irish Pub."

"Yes, Son. Very good. We'll stay there for a while. It's a good little place."

He pulls in perfectly to the parking spot in front. I stare straight ahead. Everything is almost numb. Not much of anything moving. Not much of anything happening. I get out, and the sky is turning its dark blue.

Dad opens the door and walks in with the walk I know. He knows this place.

The long, shellacked bar to our right, small chairs and tables to the left, and the narrow entrance make everything seem tight. Fifteen feet straight down, and the place opens into a wide bunch of pool tables that all tell me I don't wanna be here.

"Howdy, gentlemen. Welcome." The young black-haired bartender wipes down his counter as his eyes point at us. Dad doesn't even look at him and walks right by. Wonder if they've gotten into it.

The bartender gives Dad a nasty look.

"Sit here, Son." Dad points to the stool at the end of the bar. He sits across from me and looks to see who's shooting pool.

He looks at me, but his eyes are far away. "Arash, you want something?" We look to my left at the same time. "How about some of that pumpkin pie right there?"

"Yes." I've been eyeing those two round beauties since I got here.

"He'll take a pumpkin pie, please. Thank you," Dad says, keeping his eyes on the players.

The bartender waits for Dad to actually look at him, gets irritated, looks at me, gets nice, and smiles. "One slice coming up for the young fellow."

I look up and wonder what the heck I'm doing here.

This slice of pumpkin pie is like heaven sitting in front of me. The crust is almost perfect except for the tiny piece that cracked off, probably when it was being sliced. I almost don't wanna touch it. But before I know it, I shovel it down. Nothing but a few sad crumbs left.

"Want another piece?" Dad nods at my empty plate.

"Mm-hmm."

"Just tell the man and he will give it to you." Dad's gotten deep into the players, sorting out who's a hustler and who's the sucker. On a normal night, he'd easily pull the sucker in for $20 a rack, even $50. Or maybe he'd challenge the hustler for top dog in the joint. Sometimes he'd lose. Mostly, he wins. Not tonight. He's too scared, and barely hiding it.

Me too. I chug some ice water, hoping something will help. What did he say Shelby said? I should ask him exactly, but will he get scared, or more sad, or freak out? "Hey, Pop, why did Shelby say she'll call Child Protective Services?"

He turns to me like someone just shot him. He doesn't answer. He looks at the floor and his brain gears turn. He looks up and pretends to watch the players. He scoots over next to me, rubs his eyes with his palms, and he's so heavy it's like he's going to crash through the floor and get sucked to the earth's core at any second. "I fucked up, man." He looks at the ceiling, the side, and back at me. "I said some shit to her, you know. I got hot. I called her a bitch and cursed her for some stupid shit—I don't even remember what the fuck it was. Then she said some things that made me more angry—you know, provoked me and shit. And I fuckin' blew up on her—screaming and shouting. I said, 'You can't say that shit to me!' Then she went crazy, man. I shouldn't have said what I did. Next thing I fuckin' know, she's saying she's had enough of this shit, she's tired of all of it, and she's gonna kick me out. I told her to go fuck herself and that the house is my house, and I will kick *her* the fuck out. Then she got so angry, like a volcano, man, and she told me I better get the fuck out and that she is gonna call Child Protective Services and tell them I was allowing drunks, drug users, and dangerous people to be in the presence of a minor—you. She also said that she would tell them I have been neglecting and abandoning a minor—that some nights I would leave to sleep in another house, which you and I have agreed on, but that CPS, man—they could take legal action on that shit and maybe take you away from me, for real. That look in her eye—I fuckin' believed her. I knew she could do it. She went crazy and shit. So I got the fuck out of there. I come grabbed you, and now we send you to California for the time being. I ain't fucking letting no one touch you, man. Fuck that shit—no one is taking you away from me."

CHAPTER TWO

Hiding Fear

Death's door is dark brown. I don't want to turn this faded brass door-knob, no sir. I mean, that two-hour walk was awesome—the way the grass was smiling at the water drops sitting on each blade, the trees that woke up before I got there, and the sun that was getting ready to blaze me on fire—and now I gotta walk into this freakin' place?

I hope he's not upset. If he finds out I was out that long without telling him, he might blow his top and want to kill me. 8:15 a.m. says trusty Mr. Casio calculator watch. Maybe he's asleep. God, let him be asleep. Gonna have to walk in ninja style, Arash. Can't have him angry and exploding all over the place—not today. It'll ruin the whole thing and everything great about Saturdays. Let him not scream at me, Sis, or Stepmom today.

"Chck, chck, eeeh!" This knob and these dang hinges need some lube, dude. I open the door just enough to stick my neck in. My heart squashes down like a pancake, squeezed flat, and my throat freezes tight into a thin string that no sound dares squeak out of. Gotta make sure there's no one in there. Any more scared, and my body will start shaking, like when they bully us at school, threaten to take our lunch money, and I start wanting to fight them.

I look down the center hallway and all around. No one. No disaster. Left leg in, right leg in, and my sneaker touches the always-dirty-looking, yellowish linoleum tiles like a whisper touches the wind. Everyone's probably still asleep. My gut tightens harder. I can't disturb anyone, not even one bit. If I do, everything will be my fault. I'll be the worst person in the whole world.

A few tip-toe steps, and I stretch my neck left and into the kitchen—dark as a dungeon as usual. Our trusty monster-sized chain sits through the fridge's top and bottom handles with its lock on to make sure nobody steals the other guy's food. All is well. It's a western ghost town in here—quiet, dead, and where the slightest one thing, moves everything.

To my right, across the kitchen, and down a short hallway, my ears make a quick right, go down a bit, and land at Sis's door. Seems quiet there too.

Back to business. I walk down the main hallway more, smooth as butter, and I'll be good. Mac's room on the left—just past the kitchen—is quiet too. Those late-night sessions with that super-hot girlfriend of his probably got them dead tired—I mean, the loud-as-heck slapping sounds coming outta there at all hours, day and night, are crazy. The dude's gotta be tired. And that cheap-ass, hollow and paper-thin brownish door that Dad slapped on when constructing his room doesn't help any of our ears from the madness.

A few more steps and Bret's room is on the left, down from Mac's. Another Dad-built, brown-door room to rent, that sits where our living room should. His door always seems a deeper quiet somehow. Who knows where Dad found him, but he's like an angel—super nice and unbelievably kind. Works with NASCAR or something and spends some nights in a trailer near the track. Wonder if he slept there last night. Sounds like it, from the dead quiet of nobody's home. He's one of my favorites. Even if he was here and he happened to accidentally stroll out, he'd be cool and wouldn't do anything to get Dad on my case. He understands me with his eyes. I like that about him.

All right, Pops, I'm coming past your door on the right. Let nothing stir anything near you, and may you just stay quiet. Quiet now, and I'm almost through and to my room straight ahead, at the end of the hallway, just ten feet past yours. Man, I wish you didn't trash our living room to make the dough you want. I stop. His double white doors don't seem to want to move, even with the tinniest breath of someone awake in there. But what if I'm wrong? Can't think straight. If he hears me, it'll be like getting caught trying to escape the castle and getting thrown into the dungeon to die. Eight years old is too young to croak. Stay in, Pop—do that resting thing you like to do in your bed, where you just lay there, 'cause God knows you don't freakin' sleep. That army stuff when you were young, with all the forced waking drills at all hours of the night, messed you up good—I think you're right. So relax now with your wife, Shelby, and everything is gonna be cool. Do not even think about coming out here to hassle me.

I focus back on my room. A few more steps and . . .

"Arash! That you, man? Fuck you doin' in the hallway?"

Freak! Does this guy has some super Spidey-sense or what? I stay frozen, but I'm freakin' out. My throat grabs tight, and my hands and feet go ice cold. I don't wanna say a word. Just stay behind your closed doors, stay cool, and don't come out. "Hey, Pop! Um, I'm here!" I match his yelling and stop dead to listen if he's walking my way.

"Fuck you go, man? This shit is early in the morning!"

"Uh . . . just for a walk! Going back to my room! Going to rest!" I make a goofy face and sarcastic smile. In my imagination, I slap him in the face for bugging me. And stop with the zillion questions, Jake.

"Okay, man. You know, that is a good idea! Go and rest now in the meantime!"

Now keep your mouth shut, Arash. Just go, nice and quiet to your room, chill, close the sliding glass door behind you, and sit on your bed.

A few steps, slide and click, and it's closed. "Uhhhhh, hahhhhh." A deep breath sucks itself in and out of my lungs, and my shoulders drop like two bags of sledgehammers. Finally! So happy to be home in my beautifully large, rectangular Florida room. Even if Dad built it right on top of our backyard—I don't care. It's massively big, I can rest here, and nobody bothers me.

I cannonball jump, my back slam-bounces on my mattress top, and I stretch out long from head to toe. The sun tries to fill the room and touches my body some. The shadows on the ceiling as I stare at them want to stretch out and touch the whole world. Everything's so quiet, so peaceful.

CHAPTER THREE

Heart Friend

Bang, bang, bang, bang, bang!

"Arash! Somebody is knocking on the fucking door, man!"

This guy. Does he ever not scream, or ever take a breath between his words? I'm not moving. The sun warming my legs all over is so nice. I maybe have a few seconds before he bitches again.

Bang, bang, bang!

Shoot.

"Arash, man—what the fuck! Get that shit! Say something so I know you can hear me! I'm not getting that shit! You get it. I am resting now. If it's Mark and he doesn't have my money, tell him I'm going to fuck his shit up, and he better have my money and deliver it now, or I'm going to get hot, man! Tell him I won't stand for that shit, and if he doesn't have it, I am coming for his ass!"

"Are you sure you don't wanna get it? You can tell him yourself!" I scream from my room through the small opening of my door. I hold my breath, squeeze my lips together, and bug my eyes out as I smile to myself. I bet he's too tired to get pissed at me for messing with him though.

"Arash, man!" he belts out loud. His breathing is getting weak. "Don't fuck with me now. You go."

Oh, he's tired. "Okay, Pop. I'll get it!" I laugh as I sprint Bruce Lee–fast down the hallway and open the door quickly.

"Hey, Arash. What's up?"

"Jimmy! What's up?"

Slap, whack, thump, bump, and our hands pull away from each other in the most excellent handshake of all time. I smile huge. He nods with a small smile.

"Everything cool, Jimbo? Whatcha doing here so early? Dude, it's gotta be like nine."

"Yeah. Just went for a walk and seeing what you up to." His straight, rusty-red hair looks like it has the slightest layer of dust all over it as it sits there, still as stone. I like the way it's cut straight across his forehead while the back is longer down to a pointed tail, about mid-neck long. His whitish-red forearms say they'll burn super easy in the hot sun, and they do, and his palms are as thick and dry as a lizard's. But my favorite shorter-than-me, freckled-all-over, sniffling friend is here, and that's all I care about.

"Come in, come in." My smile stays miles wide as he strolls in.

He wanders into the kitchen, picks up the pepper shaker, looks at it, and looks back up at me.

"Wanna walk around?"

"Yes! Of course!" I turn my palms up as I scrunch my lips. "Dad! Can I go with Jimmy outside?"

"Sure, Son. Go!" he screams from his room.

"He's probably happy to get me out of the house so he doesn't have to deal with me doing crazy stuff and getting bored."

"Ha." Jimmy lowers his head and keeps his eyes pinned on me as if to say, "What the hell you gonna do with that guy?"

"Okay! Bye, Pop!"

"Wanna walk over to the Sev?" Jimmy's brown eyes wait forever for what he knows I'm gonna say.

"Pshh, hell yeah! Let's go! When would I turn down going to our favorite 7-Eleven?"

He nods and turns, and we walk together as if to get as far away from any parent, or living place of any parent, as possible.

We bust a left down my street, and at about six houses away, we're all good.

"Your parents cool?" I look at him.

"I don't know, dude. They had this huge fight last night, and I just wanted to get out of the house this morning. I never know how things are going to be—good or bad—after one of those."

"I know how that goes, dude. Sometimes it's too crazy in my house. What did they fight about? Did they say you did something wrong again?"

"I don't even know. It's like I'm always doing something wrong."

"Yeah, I get it."

"But I don't even think it was me this time—most of it seemed like they were just angry with each other."

"They probably were, dude." Mm, I don't wanna say something that'll make him stop talking or upset him. Try to say the right things, Arash. Try to keep him with you. "Uh, yeah—you should hear the shit that goes on in my house, bro. People getting crazy on Friday and Saturday nights. This one dude, just last week, punched through the wall 'cause he was angry at I don't know what, and then these other two guys got into a fight over a girl and beat the shit out of each other—I mean, blood everywhere!"

Jimmy looks at me, and his eyes widen at the craziness I just said. And then a second later, he looks down at the side of the asphalt road for small pebbles to kick. He doesn't care about Dad's lunatic tenants.

"And then sometimes he gets so angry at Orly. He really gives it to her. He shouldn't."

Jimmy perks up fast. "He hits her?"

"Sometimes. Sometimes he hits me too. It's really hard to watch with her though. Sometimes I have to go out, just do something else."

Jimmy's eyebrows pop up, and then he goes back to the pebbles on the ground. "Hey!" He pops straight up like he just got electrocuted. "Wanna go roller-skating this Saturday?"

"Oh heck yeah! That would be awesome, dude!"

"Don't forget to bring your jacket."

"Definitely. How else we gonna do those backspins good?"

"Yeah!" Jimmy turns to me with a hand up, ready to smash me a high five. "Snap!" Our palms crash for the whole block to hear. "Breakdancing is the best. I really love it. I've been working on this Dead-Man Drop. You swing one leg forward, then whip it back as fast and hard you can so it flips your whole body backward and you can land on your back. You have to make sure you land flat on your back and keep one knee bent so you'll be posing right."

"Holy crap. That's gotta knock the wind clean out of you."

"No, you just breathe out when you land so that doesn't happen."

"You're crazy, dude. I ain't doin' that shit."

We bust out laughing.

"But seriously, after we break, if you do too many of those, are you still gonna be able to skate and play video games and hit on chicks?"

"Dude, don't you worry about me. I've been practicing. And I need to talk to those girls—you know how it is."

"I know how you are, dude. You don't need to tell me."

"Ha ha ha." We look at each other.

I can't wait for this weekend. I'm bouncy and could almost glide down this sidewalk, around the next block, up a few houses, and around the corner to the Sev, like I'm floating on air itself.

CHAPTER FOUR

Mystery Sister

Knock, knock.

Her door squeaks open. "Orly?" I stick my head in. "You there? What you up to?" Her eyes catch mine, and then she goes back to doing what she was, sitting there on her bed, across the room from me. She flips through papers like she's trying to find something in a hurry. She doesn't look too good, and she doesn't look like she's gonna answer anytime soon. "Uh, you okay?"

"Ah! Where the fuck is it?" She throws the papers down on her mini fridge at the foot of her bed, then jumps up and shoots to her closet across the room, right next to me.

I scoot left, just behind her, but in front of her dresser, pretending not to be in the way. Stevie Nicks sits posing on a chair–black lace, leggings, and eye shadow. Nobody else wears black punk the way she does. Orly loves her like a psycho—I like that. My eyes drift to my left. Hanging from about the same height and right next to Orly's closet, AC/DC stares at me like a bunch of maniacs. Dude, I don't know what she sees in those guys though.

Orly jumps out from sifting through clothes. "Uh!" She jumps back in and continues hunting. Yeah, she's definitely not happy.

"You okay, Sis?" I turn to look at her.

"Everything's fine." She's super pissed.

My eyes peek to my side to watch her. I want to look over and tell her light brown eyes she doesn't have to worry; they're usually nice to me. Her bouncy bunch of reddish-brown, tightly curled hair, that when it gets wet pulls down to her waist, bings and bops wherever she goes with a teeny delay. Her skin is gentle and smooth—a pretty doll white when she's not tanning a lot. I like it like this—pretty as ever. Her cheeks have more rosy pink in them today, probably cause she's fussing around. Don't stare too much, Arash, or she'll notice and get irritated. Gosh, I wish she had time to hang out today.

"So what do you want?" The top half of her is waist-deep in the closet, and her knees and legs are sticking out.

I look down at the floor to where she is. "Nothing. Just seeing what you're up to. And looking at your posters."

"What? You suddenly like music?"

"Nah."

She keeps darting through the clothes in closet at hyper speed. Her tank top and shorts combo says she's probably going to hang with Michelle or some other cool friends in that group. Where *does* she get that skin from? Maybe Mom. My real mom. I look down at the dresser under Stevie and at Mom's tiny picture sitting there.

"How old was I when we left?"

"You know the story. Like, four and a half."

"Mm-hm." I do. But I need to hear it again. It's like I can never hear it enough. I dip my head to look closer at Mom, into her face, her hair, her eyes and what they want to say. Yup, Mom's skin sure is light. I look at my forearms—at least a few shades darker, like Dad's. Why don't I remember her so good—what she said, what she was like? "Hey, Orly, you remember Mom good?"

"What? Of course I do. What are you talking about?"

"This picture of her." I point at it.

"Don't forget, you were so small when Dad took us away. I doubt you can remember much."

"What was she like? What kinds of things did she say?"

"Mom? She was amazing! She was beautiful, like a model—and her legs, oh my gosh—so long and so pretty. I have more pictures. Oh my God! She loved you so much. She and I kissed you all over nonstop when you were a baby. I'd slobber all over you. You were like the love of her life. I swear I don't think she loved anyone or anything more than you. She took you everywhere with her. She loved you crazier than crazy, like to heaven and back. I should've been jealous, but I wasn't—not at all." Orly pauses, looks at me, slows down, and smiles.

My chest suddenly grabs, and my eyes start to fill. I don't want her to see me cry. She doesn't have time, and I don't want to bother her. I walk to the opposite side of the room, stand in front of another poster, and pretend to look at it. I wipe my eyes quickly, hoping that she doesn't see and that they dry miracle fast. I breathe in a strong sniffle, praying that she doesn't ask about it either. Don't constantly sniffle, Arash—she might get sad and upset. Let her be how she wants and go have fun with her friends.

"You okay?" All her moving sounds stop, and it's like she's looking at me.

Is she waiting for an answer? The room becomes quiet all around me. I have to say something. Keep your back to her, Arash. Don't give any hint of sadness. She shouldn't know. "Yeah, um, just looking at the corner of this poster, uh, making sure it's not torn."

CHAPTER FIVE

Becoming a Man

"Look at that goofy ass with the curly hair. What a dork. Does he even know where he is?"

"Ha ha ha." They both laugh.

"Dweeb. Where's he from, anyway?"

"Who cares? He's a freak, that's for sure."

"He's nobody!"

My guts start boiling. They're laughing too loud, and everyone is staring. William and his punk friend Rick—they're always making fun. Just keep looking to the side, Arash. Don't look at them; it'll just make them crazier. I sneak a peek at William, death stare him, and turn away.

"What the fuck are you looking at, you little shit? Want to make something of it?" He jumps to stand in front of his seat, bulging his chest out like he's gonna come to the back of the bus and kick my ass.

I hope that ugly green, plastic-covered bench seat with barely enough room to walk in and out trips his ass and he falls down, making a fool out of himself. Fuckers. Thank goodness my stop is almost here. I'll grab my bag last minute and dart out the back door as soon as it opens, and they'll forget about me.

"First Street!" The bus driver looks in her rearview to make sure no one is sleeping.

"Eeer, kshh." I pop up, jet down the steps, and hop on the sidewalk.

William and his buddy grab their bags and dart out right behind me. "Where do you think you're going?"

They're behind you, Arash. If you ignore them, maybe they'll just stop. I'll play it cool, not look behind me, and keep walking. I can hear their steps behind me. Just keep looking ahead. Don't mind them.

"Ping! Snap! Pop!"

"Ow!" The back of my head stings like a needle after something hits it and thumps off like a freakin' mini grenade.

A quick look back, and Will is cocking his arm to chuck another one. I see all the little orange seeds on the floor near their feet that have fallen from the branches. Some barely miss. Rick picks up a bunch and hands some to Will, and they chuck them at me.

I start running with Mr. Hundred-Pound Backpack crashing down on me with every step.

They start running, too, and throwing nonstop.

"Ow! Stop! Stop!"

"Pop! Ping! Ding!" The round beads sting my head, arms, and backpack as I run, getting nowhere.

"Ha ha ha. Get outta here! And we never want to see your bitch ass again!"

I'm almost at the corner, and the pellets stop. I slow down and look behind me—the two bozos have turned back. Suddenly, tears start pouring.

I slowly walk, crying, down the two blocks home.

I want to fall into and through the front door. My backpack smashes to the floor.

Dad suddenly appears in the hallway, like he just teleported. "Hey, man! What is that commotion?"

Crying with big gasps, I can't catch my breath. Take it easy, Arash. Slow down and tell him everything.

Right away, he sees me crying and walks over. "Hey, Son." He gently comes and holds my cheek with his palm. "What happened, man? Why you crying so hard?" He dips his head low to see my eyes and lifts my chin up to see even better, not missing even a millimeter of me.

"Got off the bus . . . uh, uh, and these two boys were right behind me, uh, uh . . . fifth graders. They started picking up seeds from the ground, and, uh, started throwing them at me as hard as they could. I ran, Dad, I ran. They just kept throwing them at me, and laughing." I cry, sucking in breaths, deeper and deeper, as my shoulders hop up and down.

"Come inside. Come sit with me now." He puts his arm around my shoulder and pulls me in, and we go to sit on his bed. I lean into him and cry more. He's silent for a second. I can almost hear his heart hurting. He squeezes me closer.

I'm really glad he's here.

"I do not like that shit, man," he says, hard, tough, and also like the gentlest thing ever. "I do not like it one bit. Tomorrow, we go and change that. Tomorrow, we help."

CHAPTER SIX

Punch and Kick, Baby

"Arash, come in. Don't be shy, standing out there like that."

I look up at the sign: "Park's Black Belt Academy," it reads. Under it, centered and perfect, in smaller letters reads: "Tae Kwon Do." My right eyebrow pops up as I look over the whole place from just inside the doorway. Dad says it's always good to be suspicious. Some kind of white, canvas-covered, wall-to-wall mat with its edges roped down covers the entire practice area. Kids of different ages with different-colored belts are jumpin' all around while one kid with a black belt tells them what to do. Some practice kicking drills with each other. A big American flag and another country's flag hang along the long rectangular wall above the wall-to-wall mirrors. A long, black training bag hangs all alone near the back corner, waiting to be smash-kicked; I like it.

"Arash, Arash, come quick. I want you to meet Master Park."

Dad is shaking hands with the head guy, I think. He looks about Dad's height—five foot seven—and is beefy, with jet-black straight hair that covers a little of his left eye. I think I like this guy. His white uniform is much thicker and cooler than everyone else's. Ooh, that black belt is worn at the edges, clean down to the white fabric underneath. Super cool. Maybe he is good. That belt's been around a while, that's for sure. I'd like to have me one of those.

"Master, please meet my son, Arash." Dad puts his hands together, prayer-like, and bows toward the master in that fake way I can't stand. "Arash, shake hands with the Master." Dad flips his head and eyebrows toward the Master, telling me to do what he says and to do it fast.

Before my hand is fully out, it's quickly sandwich-squashed by Master Park's pudgy, soft, and really warm hands. He smiles big and warmly as if to hug me with his warmth.

"Hello, Arashi. I am Master Park. Welcome." He keeps smiling like he can't stop.

"Master Park, I spoke to you yesterday, and my son wants to learn how to defend himself. He wants to try hard and do a good job. I hope that you will accept him as a student." Dad fake bows.

I swear, Dad, if you do that again, I'm gonna have to tae kwon . . . whatever your ass.

"Of course." The master dude nods at Dad and orders something to one of the students, and everyone suddenly forms two lines. His hair swings and flows, following even the teeniest bit of his head, as he reaches to his right and grabs a crisp uniform off the shelf. "Arashi, take this dobok and go try in bathroom. I tie your belt when finish." He holds his karate-chop hand straight out and points it to the back of the room across from the kickbag. He smiles and nods.

I hop, almost floating across the springy mat.

This bathroom is tiny. I look at the uniform in my hands. "Size 0.

Made in Korea," the neck tag says. So perfectly folded—so pure, clean, and white. It's right in every way. I don't want to unwrap it. I just want to keep it perfect, forever. I put on the pants, then the top. It's like someone just put the stiffest, most crumpliest thing over my body that could stand up on its own. I smile at it, and myself.

"Here!" Master Park points me in front of him as I jog out. He whips me around, reaches around to my belly while watching over my shoulder, and pins the creased center of the white belt to my belly button. He pulls the belt ends around me and crosses them behind my back, then to the front again, and ties a knot so fast and hard that either he's gonna crush me or pull the belt ends clean off. Neither happens. But it makes the funnest, zippiest-sounding, fabric-on-fabric sound I like.

"You like it?" Dad looks at me with a bright face.

"It's cool!"

"Looks great, Son."

Master Park puts his hand on my back. "Arashi, how old you are?"

"Eight years old, Mr. Park."

"Son, that's Master Park."

"Oh, sorry, Master Park." I smile.

"No problem!" The master waves his hand in the air like it's absolutely nothing. He puts his hand on my shoulder. "You tall for your age." He looks at Dad, then back at me. "Good. But little bit skinny." He looks me up and down with a sharp eye. "Make punchi fist."

I put my right hand into a fist and hold it in front of him.

Master Park takes it, turns it, and especially inspects my knuckles. "Good punchi fist. We make Arashi more stronger." His eyes sparkle a happiness I'm not too sure is real, and he smiles widely. "Joy, please come here. Please practice together with Joy. Joy, horse stance, basic punchi, basic *ap chagi*, front kick."

"Yes, sir!" she screams me into deaf land.

I rub my ears.

Her eyes jump on me. "Hi, I'm Joy!" She and her long, wavy brown hair bounce all over.

"Hi." I look her up and down. Blue belt, huh.

"Wanna stretch a little?"

"Okay."

"Just do what I do. It's pretty easy." She puts her hands on her knees, squats down, stretches one leg to the side, looks back, and smiles bigger at me than she should. Dad always says to watch out for people when they're a little wacky or too nice. They usually want something from you. I watch her close and follow her close too.

"Okay, everybody line up! *Chariot! Kunyeh!*"

Joy and I watch from the corner as everyone bows to the flag and then to the Master. Joy does it, too, and I follow.

"So that meant, 'Attention! Bow!' Okay, that's good for stretching. Let's go into horse stance now and do basic punching."

"What does your blue belt mean?"

"Oh, it means . . . like, I'm halfway there."

"Halfway where?"

"To black belt. So it's white, yellow, green, blue, brown, red, black. But it takes longer between belts the higher you go."

I nod and look her over once more.

"Back to horse stance, and then fighting stance for the front kick. Okay, so each time you punch or kick, you have to *kee hap*."

"Kee-what?"

"Ha ha. It's like a yelling that sounds like 'kee-yah!' You have to say it as loud as you can. It's good spirit. You'll get the hang of it. Just stand right behind me and do what I do."

I do. And I smile.

She turns around to me often, watching how much I bend my knees and if I'm doing it right enough. I try to copy her as perfect as I can.

Master Park walks by like a general, hands behind his back, and looks me over. "Good job."

Before I know it, we join the lineup and bow, and class is over. I look over to the chairs near the entrance, and Dad must have snuck in at some point. He's sitting with some other parents. He stands as I come close.

"Good job, Son." He puts his soft hand on the back of my shoulder, looks me dead in the eye, and half smiles.

"That was fast. Was that an hour?"

"Yeah, man. You did a lot."

Master Park comes over, puts his hand on my shoulder, looks at me, and then looks at Dad. "Good job! Now coming back tomorrow with Daddy. More practice." He almost giggles as he rubs my long-in-all-directions curly brown hair.

We wave goodbye.

"How did you like that, man?"

"I liked it, actually." My eyebrows hop up.

"Good, man. We come tomorrow again. I signed you up, and you can come up to six days a week. This will be great for you." We walk out, and he points to the right, across the big dirt lot. "Look, our house is so close—just across there and two houses to the right. You can walk over after school every day. He looks up, across the sky, and back to the clump of keys in his hand."

We head to the car.

I look at our house across the lot. "You think this will help, Dad?" I look up at him.

"Help with what?"

"You know, help with me. The whole bus thing—when they shipped a bunch of us off to another school—desegregation, they said it was. And getting beaten up by those two kids on the bus from my own school. You know, yesterday!" My stomach starts scrunching hard, and I'm about to give him two funny looks. So annoying when he makes me repeat things. Isn't he paying attention? Like, ever!

"Oh, that shit? Yeah, man. That is why I brought you here. Nobody is going to beat up my son. You have to learn how to defend yourself and kick some ass when the time comes. This shit will do it. Just stay and practice. Put hard work into it, and you'll be the one kicking asses next time. Ha ha ha."

CHAPTER SEVEN

Lovesick

"**H**ey, Pop."

"Hey, Son. Nice to see you. Fuck you doing sitting in the kitchen here in the dark all by yourself? Turn the light on."

"Just sitting for a few minutes." I like the dark sometimes. And it's quiet too. Nobody thinks to bother you when they walk into a dark room.

"Ha ha ha." He turns the light on and plops two grocery bags down on the table that make thumping sounds as things bounce inside. "Look here, man, I found the most beautiful melons you ever saw in your life-time." He digs into a bag and lifts one up like it's made of pure gold. "Look at this beauty. I found these cantaloupes, and I could not pass that shit up." He closes his eyes, pushes his nose into its skin, and takes a breath so deep, he could pull the skin clean off. "You can smell how sweet it is . . . ahh!" He shoves it into my nose.

I sniff.

"This is going to be so sweet and delicious. You will see."

"How many did you get?"

"Shit, you know they had to double bag it, man. Ha ha. I got about nine of these motherfuckers." He opens the bag wide for me to see. "See how gorgeous and perfect?"

"That's a lot of melons."

"No problem, man. Don't you worry about that. You know—we used to eat these when I was a kid. We would slice them, put them on ice, and eat them in the hot summer sun with feta cheese and thick, chewy *barbari* bread baked fresh. Yes, that was good times. Let's eat some together now, you and your father. You try cantaloupe with me." He smiles sweetly. He quickly stabs the cantaloupe in the center and cuts it clean in half.

"Take it easy, Pop. You're going to take your fingers off."

"Ha ha ha. You have to make sure you scoop the insides out and all that." He cups the slippery seeds and center stringy things in his hand and disgustingly flicks them into an empty bag. His hands drip slimy goo from the plate to the bag and all over.

He gives me the knife, and I repeat, except more slowly and with no goo.

A whiff of the super-sweet smell pops out. "Hey, you're right. These things smell pretty amazing. Is that how you know it's going to taste sweet?"

"Yes, man, I told you that shit. Now that you have a slice, turn the knife horizontal to the table, slip it between the skin and orange inside, and slice carefully, till it's split. Don't cut your fingers and shit. Then you slice it vertically into cubes." He then jabs a cube with his knife tip, puts it in his mouth, and slides the knife out like he's done it a zillion times.

"Right off the knife, Dad?"

"Yeah, man. Eat like a man, but don't be stupid—use some common sense and pay attention. Don't cut your tongue or lip when you pull that shit out. You know, most people don't use their common sense. Most people are stupid, man."

"Oh, my gosh," I mumble, with melon juiciness wanting to pour out uncontrollably. "This is amazing."

"See, man, I told you. You learn from your father. We will eat this beautiful and delicious cantaloupe melon together." He slurps and chews too fast for juice not to leak out the side of his mouth.

Gross. I watch him plow through melon number two before I've eaten even a few slices.

"Hey, Pop, are these smaller than usual?"

"Yes, man. A little smaller. Usually, they are bigger than this and I can't pick one up just grabbing it from the top. But this one I can."

I cut open my second. "Dad, is that your third already?"

"That is no problem. You take your time. I am happy that you are hungry, man. I like that shit."

"It's easy with these. They're delicious."

He nods, mumbles, and chews.

Two and three-quarters of a melon through, and . . . "Uh! I'm gonna explode, Pop. That's almost three for me, and I can't eat another bite."

He leans over and examines my plate. "That's not bad, man—two and a half cantaloupes for you is all right. Okay, you rest for the meantime. I will finish now."

I take a deep breath and stare at the cantaloupe skins on my plate, the four destroyed ones on his, and the fifth he's about to polish off. Maybe it's like what Mom said when I was a kid: The more you eat, the stronger you'll be. If that's true, then he's the Hulk.

"You know, man, I do love that shit." He plows through another slice.

"Hey, Pop, I'm tired. I think I'm gonna lay down and take a nap."

"Yes. That is a good idea to take a nap and recharge in the afternoon. That will be good for you." He smiles small.

Standing up is a stomach disaster. So full. Please let lying down help. My bed never looked so good. Just need to sleep.

Suddenly, I shake awake. "Bloop, bloop, bloop, bloop." Uh, my stomach! I look at the clock: 8:42 p.m. Night is starting to come through the windows. Oh, stomach, just stop so I can go back to sleep–please . . . till morning. "God, I'm sorry I ate too many cantaloupes. I won't do it again. Just make this pain stop and let me sleep through the night."

My eyes pop open. Only forty minutes of sleep, but it seems like pain forever. "Bloop, bloop. Bloop, bloop, bloop." Uh, nothing is any better. "Ahh!" I sit up. It's gurgling and hurting everywhere. Just close your eyes, Arash–maybe it'll go away. Go back to bed and try not to think about anything.

"Ow! Ow!" I jump and run as fast as I can to the bathroom and jam my face in the bowl. "Blaaaa! Blaaaa!" Thank goodness I got here just in time and didn't puke on the–"Blaaa!" The waves of pain! I want to disappear somewhere far away. No more. I rest my head on the bowl between upchucks. Oh, someone please make this stop. I'm gonna die now for sure. "Blaaaa." Freaking cantaloupe.

"Bam, bam, bam, bam!"

"Uhhhh."

"Arash, man. Is that you?" Dad cracks the door open and sticks his head and shoulders in. "Oh shit! What the fuck, Son?"

My hand barely holds up my falling-down head. "Mmmhhh."

"What happened, man? You vomiting? Sick and shit?" He looks around.

"Ahhhh. Blaaaa!"

He looks over my head and into the bowl. "That fucking cantaloupe. How long has this been going on, man?" He kneels, puts a hand on my shoulder, and lets me vomit everything. When I sit back, he wipes my face and pulls me into him.

"Few minutes." I close my eyes and curl into a ball. Just a bit here and I'll be okay, maybe. Somewhere under this almost dying, I'm so happy to have Dad. He's my best help.

"You got fucked up, man. Come on, we're getting you to the hospital. I will lift you up." He does from under my arms. He walks me beside him to the car and sits me in.

"I'll put the window down for a little fresh air, and that will be good for you. Just relax now for the time being."

My head leans against the door's side, and I want to erase this whole day. God, please come help and just shoot me to the end when I'm perfect.

We pull in, and before I know anything, I'm lying down on one of their beds. Dad sits beside me, his knee bouncing fast, as he rolls his house keys through his fingers.

"Hi there, I'm Dr. Dirk. Are you Arash?"

I nod.

"Sir, this your son?"

"Yes, Doctor, sir. This is my son, Arash. My name is Jake, and he is a very good boy."

"Please tell me what happened."

"Yes, sir. Well, you know, at approximately twelve thirty yesterday afternoon, we ate some cantaloupes. They were on the smaller side and . . . well, this morning, I found him in the bathroom vomiting what looked like all of the cantaloupes. He said he also was a little bit warm when he woke up, but he did vomit a lot. I think that's all of it, sir."

"I see. And how much cantaloupe are we talking here?"

"Well, he ate about two and a half cantaloupes, to be honest with you."

"Two and a half cantaloupes! Is that right, Son?"

"Uh-huh." I nod, curled up on my side. Thank goodness they have this bed 'cause if this guy asks me to sit up, forget it.

"You know, Doctor, sir, they were on the smaller side, but still maybe it was too much, yes."

The white-coat doc looks me over good, leaves, and then comes back.

"Son, could you please sit up and drink this small cup of water?"

Are you out of your mind? I'm gonna vomit just looking at it. I sit up. "It'll come up," I say in a weak voice, trying to keep my eyes on him.

"I understand. Please drink it anyway." He puts a white tub on my legs. "This is just in case you need it."

I hold it with one hand and drink the small cup. One, two, three—"Baaaa!" right back into the tub. Dad takes it from me, and I lie back.

The doc takes out his prescription pad and jots something. "Looks like food poisoning. He should be able to drink in a few hours. Mr. Jacob, please take Gatorade and dilute it to one-half strength with water, and give him a little to drink every fifteen to twenty minutes or so for the first few hours. Start small and build up to half a glass, not going too fast, until he can hold it down and starts to pee regularly. It could take until tomorrow. I wrote the directions here." He hands the slip to Pops.

"Yes, sir, Doctor, sir. I will do that. Thank you very much." Dad holds the prescription like it's gold, puts his palms together in a prayer pose, and bows.

CHAPTER EIGHT

Who's Gonna Pay Rent

I speed fast, hitting the brakes to skid perfectly over the driveway and the grassy front yard, stopping dead between the two duplexes. "Hey, Pop! Hey, Pop! Gotta ask you something."

He turns to me. His face is resting easy. "Hey, man, hang on. I am talking to darling Jane here at the moment. Come stand next to me now, and I will talk to you in a minute."

Stand next to me? Wait? Who are you talking to? Me? I got some good news, and I have to share it fast—there's no waiting. My head rocks side to side. I have to jump into their conversation. Heck, what they're talking about can't be important anyway.

"Hey, Jane. You know, I know you are having trouble with Rick, but don't you worry now. Everything is going to be okay."

What? He's being nice to her? One look at Jane tells me she is dang piss drunk in the middle of the day. But, wow—is she a knockout. Her straight black hair is held up almost magically by a clip that's barely keeping it all from flopping down. Her light tan skin is perfect all over. The light freckles on her nose that spread along her cheeks—I think I'm going to die now; she's too beautiful. The way she holds her hands in the air, palms up when she speaks, and pushes her neck forward the teeniest bit to tell you something's important. I wish I could peel my eyes away from her. Her white, almost see-through tank top drapes a little in front while her lace bra makes it easy to see details. I can see why Dad wants to hold her. I want to hold her. And those super-short jean shorts with the strands dangling from the bottom edges—how they rest along her thighs while the rest of her smooth legs stretch down, may all be just too perfect.

"Ha ha. Now, Jane, you know, sweetheart, you can't let those things bother you. You and Rick have been here a long time. You live in one of my best rooms, and everything has worked out up to this point. You are my good friends now. Rick is a good guy. You tell him to come talk to me. You know I will take care of him, and I will definitely also take care of you—no problem." He winks at her. Dad's grin stays, widening as he keeps eye contact. His eyes pause at her lips, breasts, and then legs.

She can't tell. She's too drunk.

What does he want from her? Sex? Or more? His eyes say what's going to happen next. Crap. He's gonna do it—he's going to screw this one too. Don't do it, Dad. It won't be good . . . for either one of you.

"Jake, listen, I don't know if we're going to have enough for rent this week. With all the beer and cigarettes Rick is buying . . . He's also been shootin' pool and losin' money—you know, ten here, twenty there."

Something in the way her voice cracks—like she's two shades from crying but can't. I look up, deep into her eyes, and everything changes. Her eyelids can barely hold themselves up, and her words and hand movements don't work together because of the amount of beer she's probably chugged. I wish she wasn't drunk so she'd know how beautiful she was, and how perfect. Then maybe she wouldn't be so sad. I just want to hold her, talk to the sleepy part inside, and tell her everything's gonna be fine—that she'll be fine. But I don't think she could hear me. The alcohol is too thick. I want to cry and let her cry too. Don't think she has any friends—not Mr. Drunk Rick dude and definitely not have-sex-with-me-this-instant Dad. Okay, enough is enough. These two need to get the show on the road, 'cause I need to talk to Pops. And here it comes . . . Yes! She's turning away and hopefully won't turn back.

He watches her butt as it walks away, perfectly shaped and beautifully moving. He turns to me. "Your turn." He locks eyes on me. "What's up, man? I see you standing there the whole time. What's on your mind?"

"So, Jimmy invited me to the lake this Saturday with some of his family. It's gonna be a whole day in the sun and lots of fun. Can I go? Please!" My eyes want to squeeze, and my knees and forehead want to bend to the floor like those people on TV who kneel to God when all they want is for a prayer to come true.

"Yeah? You are serious, man?" His eyes wander down the block, at the grass in front of him, and then at me. They change into swords about to go through my guts if I'm lying or have the wrong answer. "Are you done with your homework?" His eyes keep burning into me.

"Well, I just got home, and I'm going to go do everything due Monday right now. I'll double-check to make sure nothing is missing and even do extra credit if there is any." Lay it on thick, Arash. He'll like that.

One eyebrow pops up as he lasers in on me. "You know that shit is important. Only if you finish your homework, you can go. Are you understanding me? Because if I find out you skipped that shit or your grades are falling, I'm gonna get hot, and you won't like that shit."

"Uh-huh." I nod strong and quick—not too quick to where it's not believable, but not too slow to not be paying attention. "I understand." I stand tall like anchors are growing through my feet and deep into the ground.

His lips scrunch together, and his eyes run me over to make sure nothing's fishy. He nods. "Yes, go if that is the case. You can go." His hand raises in a mini-twist motion that says I can go and that he's finished with me.

"Yes!" My hand clenches into a fist as I pull it fast by my side. "Thanks, Pop." I want to jump all over and hug him with everything I've got, but it's better to keep cool. I explode inside as I walk away. Stay calm and hold it together, Arash. Into the house, and I want to do cartwheels and scream, "Yoo-hoo! Yes!" That homework isn't done, and it's not gonna get done.

CHAPTER NINE

Sandwich Love

Baa! Baa! Baa! Baa!

"Uh!" I wish that alarm would shut the freak up. My head lifts and my eyelids peel back, but only the left one makes it fully open. 6:33 a.m. Those thin, red, long clock digits should really just go away. Click. Snooze it. My face slams back into the pillow. I'm never gonna get up, and Jimmy is coming at 7:30. Who sets their alarm for almost an hour before somebody comes, anyway? That's like a lifetime of sleep. My eyes close happy again. Only a few minutes, Arash. Yeah, definitely enough.

"Honk, honk!"

They're here! Yes! Grab my bag and jump outside.

There's the best Jimbo in the world—pulled right in front of the curb of my house. Jimmy's dad, in his blue Ford Bronco with the wide cream strip down the side, sits happy and bright, and his mom is riding shotgun as always. Just like I like to see. Jimmy's sitting behind his Dad. Hope he's okay. Maybe it'll be a great day.

I race to the car door. "Hey!"

"Hey." Jimmy sits straight up as I close the door behind me. He keeps his eyes glued on me. His eyebrows hop up and down. Our hands snap, slide, and grab together. He jets his neck forward between his parents and checks on them.

I watch everyone super close.

Jimmy looks at me like he's either about to cause trouble or tell me a secret. He rolls his eyes.

"Everything cool?" I whisper.

He shrugs, looks out the window and then at me, and lifts his eyebrows.

"You guys ready to go?" Mel says from the driver's seat, looking through the rearview mirror.

"Yes, Mel." Be extra nice, Arash, so everything goes smoothly.

"Hi, Arash!" Linda says in her oh-so-sweet voice as she whips her head around, slips her sunglasses up and into her bouncy red, curly hair and pins her sparkly eyes on me.

I wanna jump over, give her the biggest hug in the world, and hold on to her for a really, really long time.

"Hi, Linda." A three-quarters smile pops across my face. I turn away and smile even bigger and then look back at her.

"Mel, turn up the radio." Linda keeps her smile on me.

"Yes! Jimmy, our favorite song, 'The Coward of the County'!"

Jimmy and I start going wild, singing the heck out of the middle two verses like nobody's there and nobody cares. Linda sings with us, and even Mel taps his thumb on the steering wheel. It's a big old Bronco party. I whack Jimmy on the shoulder, and he whacks me back just a little bit harder. We sing and laugh crazy.

The song ends. "Uh, that was good." I smile and sit straight up.

Jimmy smiles back. We high-five.

"Love that song. 'The Gambler' too." I look for everybody's reaction. No one disagrees.

"Kenny Rogers is the best." Jimmy gives me the single eyebrow raise to prove he's right. "Hey, Arash, what did you do yesterday after school?"

"Not much, just came home, walked around a little, rode my bike down to the Sev, finished tae kwon do, and then busted back home to watch *Knight Rider*."

"How was tae kwon do?"

"Dude, it was pretty cool actually. I have so much to tell you about it. I think I did pretty good. And that Master Park—I think he likes me."

"That's cool. I told my parents, and they said that if you like it and it's good, they'll check it out and maybe I could go."

"Dude, that would be awesome!" My eyes bug out. "What'd you do?"

"Grounded."

"Dude, again?" I whisper, turn my palms up, and shake my head, making sure his parents don't see.

"Yeah, did some things I wasn't supposed to," he whispers.

"What? Where?"

"Just around."

"What?"

Jimmy nods, slaps his hand back and forth mid-air, and then slaps at his butt. Then, he points to his dad.

"Spanked again?" I mouth silently. I know what that's like. "Always creating trouble." I smile at him.

He pops both eyebrows up and down and starts that sneaky smile I know. We nod together.

The car slows down and pulls to the side of the road. "We're here." Mel looks at us in the rearview.

Jimmy and I look at each other and bust out through my side.

We stand along the edge of a rocky hill just outside the car.

"Hey, you two jokers, no one is leaving until you take something with you." Mel's voice hits us with its usual low-tone, serious way. Jimmy and I hop to the trunk and grab stuff.

"It's so nice out here." I look out on the whole lake as we walk the stuff down. The sunlight sparkles off its surface.

"Come on." Jimmy waves me closer to set stuff down on the picnic tables. "Mom, we're gonna go scout around."

"Okay, stay together, and don't go out too far."

Jimmy nods and jumps over to walk with me. Our steps match perfectly. He looks out at the lake, the sand under our feet, and kicks whatever's near his feet.

"You okay?" My eyes stay looking at the ground.

"Hmm." His shoulders jump. "I guess."

"Parents again? Being grounded."

"I don't know. It's like all of it, dude. Sometimes, I just don't know." He takes a deep breath, keeps looking down, and isn't interested in kicking anything.

It's like Jimmy just got punched in the gut, somehow—how sad his voice just got, like he's sucking the words he's trying to say back down and into his stomach.

It's like someone just punched me in the gut too. I stay quiet, look down, and then look at him. I hope he keeps talking, but maybe he won't.

"Hey, we can go around those bunch of trees and see if there's a way back." He comes closer to me and looks to where I'm pointing. I like it when he says yes without saying anything. "Hey, how's your dad?" He jumps and smash-kicks a sparkly rock.

"He's okay, I guess. He's usually out collecting rent or fixing stuff up. You know how he is. He talks to the tenants a lot—you know—he talks shit."

"Ha ha ha." We laugh.

"Yeah, I know that."

"I don't see him tons. I mean, he'll always pick me up from school if it's raining and when I get a flat on my bike, or if I need to go to the doctor. But, yeah, usually he's pretty busy."

"Oh, dude, I almost forgot—what happened to the school you got bussed to?"

"Oh my gosh, you'll never believe it! They just one day announced that they found asbestos in the place—the ceiling I think it was. Then they had to close the whole place down. So we just came back to school."

"That's crazy, dude." Jimmy shakes his head.

We both stop and look at the thin bunch of trees in front of us that dead-end into the hill.

"Let's head back." I look at Jimmy.

We turn together and start back, and I half smile. He's not jumping happy, but he's okay.

"Hi, boys. Back so soon?"

"Hi, Linda. Not much out there—the sandy part goes away between the cliff and the water." I point past the trees.

She smiles a giant warm one at me.

"We climbed some of the trees, too, but they're not that tall."

"I like you here with us, Arash. And I know Jimmy loves it too." She looks up and smiles through us both.

Everything in my belly and chest suddenly turns warm, like someone turned on the bubbles in the jacuzzi.

I look down for a sec and then back up. "What are you getting ready for lunch, Linda?"

"Your boys' favorite, of course—bologna-and-mustard sandwiches." She looks down and finishes spreading. I love whatever her rough-skinned little fingers make; they're so small but so pretty . . . the way she gently moves things around in the right order to set the table. I could watch it for a long time.

Mel walks up. His straight red hair, beefy arms, legs, and chest—everything around him, like a glow, says how strong he is somehow—like when Superman sucks in the sun's strength and recharges his superpowers. I bet Mel could protect Jimmy and Linda if someone ever started anything. "You boys ready for some water?" He slips his hands into his pockets. "Go get changed into your trunks. I'll bring the boat down."

"Yes!" Jimmy's eyes pop clean out of his head.

"Jimbo, dude, what the freak is he talking about? What's going on?"

"Skididdling is up first." His eyes twinkle brightly in that dangerous way.

"Ski . . . what?"

"Don't worry. Let's get changed. This is gonna be awesome!"

"Awesome for who? Awesome for you? But maybe I'm screwed." I chase after Jimmy.

"You boys ready?" Mel calls out from the boat.

"Come on, Arash. Dad backed up the boat as close as he can. We need to jump in the water and go to him."

Mel pulls us in from the water and takes us further out. "Jimmy, toss the skididdle into the water."

Jimmy flops the baby blue tube thingy overboard.

"Hey Jimmy, what kind of boat is this, and how come there's no hole in the center of that thing?" I point to the skididdle.

"See where the hole should be—it's covered with the same tough fabric as the rest, except the center dips so you can sit or lie down on it easier."

"Are you kidding me? I'm gonna sit on that thing? Dude, I'll slide right off."

"Ha ha. Now see the four handles on the top—you and me are gonna lay down crisscross." Jimmy puts his hands on top of each other, crossing them, but that does not help my freaking out one bit. "See, that's how the handles are. It's not slippery; it dips in the center more than it looks like. Wait till you get on it—you'll see. The best is, if we go crisscross, we'll have more control when Dad tries to flip us."

"Who's gonna get flipped?"

"Ha ha. Don't worry." He cannonballs off the boat.

"Wait. Dude! Jimmy. Who's gonna flip us? How?" I jump in.

"Okay, now you lay across there." Jimmy points to the top of the ski-diddle. "Here, I'll help push you on, but hold the handles."

He does.

"Now I'm gonna climb on and lie across you 'cause I'm shorter."

"You boys all set!"

"Yeah, Dad, go!" Jimmy screams. "Arash, hold on tight just like you are—strong arms, and when I say 'lean,' follow me, and lean with me into the wake. Otherwise, we'll flip."

"You didn't say nothing about no leaning and no flipping. Like flip off this thing and into the water?"

"No, like he'll flip it with us on it."

My face goes stone straight.

"Go!" Jimmy screams at his dad.

I look over the tough white handles and the million stitches keeping them on. I tug on them hard; these things will definitely hold. Suddenly we get jerked into blastoff, the skididdle yanks, and we hold on good.

I close my eyes for a sec as the boat picks up speed and hope I don't die.

"If the water is splashing your eyes too hard, turn your head the other way!"

Beboom, beboom, beboom, beboom! The bottom of this thing smacks the water hard. I think I'm gonna vomit.

Mel turns his head backward to keep an eye on us.

I'm just glad we haven't flown off. I turn my head to check on Mel. He goes even faster. My teeth clench, and I almost forget about Jimmy lying across my back.

"Yoo-hoo! Go faster!" Jimmy screams.

Oh, please shut up. I'm about to puke, and my head is jiggling all over.

"Yes! Arash, he's about to start pulling us into the side of the wake to try to flip us!"

"Okay!"

"Don't worry! Follow me! Lean into the wake with me when I say!"

I sure am glad he's screaming–this water is thrashing like crazy all around. I look to the side, and sure enough, we're getting right up to the side of the curling wave the boat makes as it plows us into another dimension. "Jimmy! The side of the skididdle is lifting up!"

"Okay! Lean into it! Toward it! Everything you got!"

The skididdle starts to lift scary on one side, but Jimmy and I lean exactly like he says–with everything we've got.

"Oh crap!"

"It's good, Arash! It's good! Keep it up!"

I open my eyes, and he's right: the skididdle is lifting high, but our leaning keeps it from flipping, barely.

Mel slows the boat, and we slide down the wake, nice and smooth. I like that.

"Ahh! Dude, that was gnarly. Ha ha. So good! Dad, you didn't get us!" Jimmy screams out to the boat.

Mel looks back at us and lifts his hand; I could swear he half smiles, but there's no way he could hear a thing.

"Arash, we did it!" Jimmy looks the happiest he's been all day.

Good for him. I slowly stop trembling and sink into the skididdle's center in a way I never thought could be so comfortable. I close my eyes, and somehow the slower smashing of the water under us is almost nice. Jimmy's body crunching me down and the spray in my eyes don't bother me one bit. My eyes shut for a second, and the sun pours down perfectly. All the scary stuff seems perfect now too.

The boat slows and we get closer to it. "Jump aboard, boys."

We grab towels and sit in the warm seats. Mel pulls us to shore.

"How'd you do, Arash?" Linda asks with a hugely happy face as she turns to see us running out of the water.

"We did great! It was pretty awesome, actually, especially when it was over. I thought we were gonna flip for sure, but Jimmy and I held on."

"Snap!" We high-five.

"All right. I like that. Here you go, boys. Your sandwiches are here, and you'll find sodas in the cooler on the floor over there. Enjoy. There's seconds if you like."

"Thanks, Linda." I grab my plate and pop over to the cooler. Jimmy and I sit on the same side of the picnic table, take bites, and look out over the water. I lift my sandwich, look at him, and smile as if we just won a championship. He lifts his, looks at me, and chews as if light is beaming from his face. I love it when he gets happy.

CHAPTER TEN

His Deeper Heart

"Fuck you doing standing here, man—just like that?"

I shrug my shoulders as I lean against the hallway next to the kitchen, as if I was standing here like a ghost, just waiting for him to come in.

"Fuck is your sister?"

"Her room."

He looks me up and down, and his eyes squint as he's trying his hardest to figure out why I've been leaning here and why I'm so calm. He nods to himself. His eyes drop to the floor, and then he looks at the front door. "Go get her. And move your asses to the car, right now."

"I nod."

Orly and I hop in, and she goes cold as she looks out the window.

"Fuck is wrong with her?" Dad cranks the engine as he looks through the rearview at me.

"I don't know." I sit straight in the back seat.

"Where we going?" Orly says.

"Visit your mom. She got sick, man. She is in the hospital."

Oh shoot, this drive is gonna be longer than long ever was.

Twenty minutes that was like three years of silence in this car, and we are free! The hospital sliding doors whip open, and that dry alcohol smell whacks me hard, along with some mixture of cleaning solution and sick people walking the hallways. I look at Dad and Orly walking ahead to the elevator.

We zoom up, walk a few rooms down, and voila: Shelby's room. Suddenly, just as we get to her door, my feet slow down. I step to the side and let Dad go in first. Sis stays behind me, her shoulder making quick friends with the wall just outside the door. She checks her nails. Sometimes I wish I had her strength—her courage to do whatever she wants, and no fear of Dad.

My eyes jump into the room. Gosh, I want to go in, but I listen, turning my head to hear what they're saying. The beeping from the machines and weak whispers from Dad don't help.

A slow step in, and my eyes stretch ahead of me, around the dividing curtain, to her toes and shins. Somehow, the thin, grandma hospital sheets have slipped off. Not me, I need my feet covered good when I'm sleeping. More steps and her gown, hands, and face suddenly appear. She's too pale to be right. Her eyes are open, but it's like they weigh a thousand pounds and will close any second. Sharp pains start in my chest, and my heart skips. What if she dies? What if she doesn't make it?

Dad holds her hand between his. He looks so softly at her—gentle and deep, like he could stay with her right here forever. The side of his eyes wrinkle, and his thin lips start smiling barely. There's a look in him—like his eyes are shaky and he's unsure of everything. His whole face wants to move into her and help. But he doesn't know what to do. He really must love her. Maybe he's given her his heart. Oh, God, please don't let her croak.

More quiet steps forward, and I see the tube taped on her arm that hangs off the bed and up a metal pole, connecting to a bag of liquid. I don't like any of this, at all.

"Come on, Son, come closer. It's all right. Hold your mom's hand now."

My legs move closer, but the rest of me doesn't want to.

"Hold her hand and tell her that you love her."

I take her other hand in mine—just like Dad. "Uh . . . I love you." I try to smile.

Her head turns to me—slow and weak.

My eyebrows lift.

She doesn't smile. She can't—she's too weak.

Me neither. I look behind me. It's Sis's turn. She snuck in and is in her signature leaning-against-the-wall pose.

"Come." Dad's hand waves her close.

Oh, but she's not coming close. That girl ain't budging. Her lifted eyebrows, interlaced fingers, and head turned away from us and to the side say she ain't doin' nothing for nobody.

Shoot!

Dad's eyes stay low. He doesn't have it in him to laser-beam kill her with his death stare or explode-scream at her today. He focuses on Shelby.

Caclunk, caclunk, caclunk, caclunk. The nurse's shoes through the doorway give her away. "Hello everyone." A bright smile and a relaxed happiness light her up, head to toe. She gently scoots past me and checks Shelby's hanging bag. She turns to us. "Hi, my name is Nurse Jenny. I'm taking care of Shelby today." She looks at us one by one. "Shelby is doing really well. Some of the medicine we've given her to calm her nerves should wear off soon, so not to worry. It would help her a lot if we could get her moving a little bit. For today, wheeling her around the hospital would be great, and soon she should be on her feet and much better in no time." She gives more smiles all around. "I'll help put her in her wheelchair, and maybe you guys take it from there."

"Yes, that is good." Dad buzzes around, looking to help with something, anything.

"Okay, Mr. Jacob, if you could just hold the handles of the wheelchair. I have the lock set on the wheel."

Dad jumps to it.

I wait, my eyes darting all over, ready to do anything or to catch anything should it fall, including Shelby.

Dad triple-checks the wheel lock. He checks one side as the nurse sets Shelby into her chair to make sure Shelby's gown doesn't get caught. He jumps to the other side to make sure everything is perfect.

Thunk. Shelby's in. She can hold her head up, but those eyes—yeah, they're not opening so good.

"Okay, Arash. Now, you come here."

I jump into place.

"Now, take her down the usual route. And you know, man, don't fucking speed and shit like you like to do. Today, take it easy, at least until she's fully awake—you know, she is fucked up at the moment from the medications and painkillers and shit. Then later you can go a little bit fast. Be careful."

"Okay. Of course." I lean close to his ear. "Dad, she gonna be okay?"

"Come here." He tugs my arms, and we go outside the doorway.

He whispers, "Sure, man, sure. You know, she has to get better. In Arabic, we say: 'Shwaya shwaya.' Slowly, slowly. For the time being, she is in the hospital, but she will get better—not to worry. Soon you will see—she will be back home, no problem."

"But what's wrong with her?"

He looks down, left, and to the right. He's trying to decide how much he should tell me and how much he thinks I should know. "Well, you know, she had in her colon some things that got a little bit inflamed, and doctors had to give her some medicine for it. Sometimes it gets a little bad, and this time she got a little bleeding, and so we took her to the hospital. Now, everything is under control, and we take care of her, all of us together. You know, that is important." Dad's eyes go funny. He's starting to get uncomfortable. Any more and he'll cry. He heads back in.

Under control? She bled? A million questions I want to ask, but he might fall down or something. I should stop. Orly's hanging back in the room. Wonder if she can even hear us. No way she's okay.

I grab the wheelchair handles with my strongest grip and missile lock onto the exit door. Can't stop thinking about how Dad was looking at her in the bed. How his eyes poured out every sadness inside him and everything he wanted to do for her.

I look left, then right, and make a right turn into the hallway, smooth and perfect.

CHAPTER 11

Mom's Gift

"**A**rash! Is that you, man? Go see your sister. She has a package for you—some shit from your mother."

Holy crap. Mom! I lean my bike against the wall, fast, and jump to Sis's door.

Knock, knock. No answer. Knock, knock, knock. I glue my ear to her door. No music, singing, or on the phone sounds. Hmm . . . "Orly! Orly!" I can't stand waiting!

"What!"

Oh, she's definitely pissed. Oh well. Not important today—I've gotta get my goodies. "Hey, Dad said I should come in and get the stuff Mom sent."

"Hold on. Give me a sec."

A sec? Girl, you've had forever since I first knocked. This door better open lickety-split cause I need to get that half a box of deliciousness coming to me.

"Come in."

I open the door. She's sitting on the edge of her bed, turned to the side, but I can see the edges of her eyes. Have you been crying?

She won't answer.

"Dad said there was a package from Mom." I look down to get a hint at what her eyes are doing. "Can I see the box?" I tilt my head low to see hers, but she bends away a little more. I take a deep breath. Why are you just sitting there, like your body has fallen through the bed and it can't move at all? So heavy.

Her pointer finger lifts up like from one of those zombie movies and points to the white bag sitting in the middle of the bed.

I go slowly to get it. Something's off. Why is she being like this? I go for the bag, and I'm so excited to see what's inside, I'm going to explode. Gotta stay cool—don't want her to be sad that I'm happy, and she's gonna if I start jumping all around.

I un-crumple the bag: two pieces of *lavashak*, the most amazing thick, chewy, sweet-and-sour dried fruit on earth; some medium pieces of *gaz*, chunks of nougat and pistachio discs of loveliness to die for covered in flour; and some knickknack candies. What? This can't be all of it. This is never all of it. Mom wouldn't send so little. Should be twice this much. My eyes start hunting around. "Orly, this all of it?"

She won't answer.

My gut starts to twist and get hot. My ears, too, and my teeth clench. My eyes need to missile lock on that brown box with the Farsi writing on it and all the international stamping. Everything is suspicious. Orly is suspicious. I eye her mini fridge, jump to it before she can stop me, and pop it open. "Aha! I knew it!" I grab the box, and it's heavy as freak—definitely a ton more than the half I got. Suddenly, I'm back in our apartment when I was five, standing in our kitchen, holding onto mom's skirt, and making her make my breakfast rice. I snap back to the box. "What the fuck!"

She snatches it away. "Get out! That's mine." She looks at the box with tears about to pour.

The fire in my gut starts burning like lava, but I hate that she's sad.

Suddenly, I bolt out. "Dad!" My scream blasts through the house. "Where are you?" I storm to his room.

He's sitting on the edge of his mattress, rubbing his forehead.

"You won't fucking believe this, Pop. Orly won't give me half of what Mom sent. That's not right, and I won't take it!" My eyes turn stone hard, and nobody on earth is going to tell me no.

"What the fuck is the commotion, man? She won't give you what the fuck?" He rubs his eyes and lifts himself like sleep hasn't left him. "Come on, man, let's go."

He knocks once and opens Orly's door without waiting. He picks the box up from the bed and hands it to me. "Take your half." He stands guard, looking around.

I hold the box and look at Orly's face that's looking to the side. I want to cry. I put the box on the bed, take exactly my half, close the top gently, and slide it just an inch closer to her. I sneak a peek at the part of her face I can see. No tears, nothing coming, but something might come soon.

As I walk out, it's like someone pancake-crushes my chest, front to back. It's hard to breathe. I stop, look in my bag, and back at her. Should I give it all back? Some of it?

CHAPTER 12

Rocket Me

Lines, lines, I hate waiting in lines. My legs wanna jump all over. "Hey, Jay, don't you hate waiting in line?"

Jay nods and gives me his cheek scrunch, which always means, "Definitely."

"Dude, so how are you so tall?" I really wanna ask him: How are you so cool and sure of everything you say, like no one can tell you different?

He shrugs and half smiles. "Wanna shoot pool at lunch?"

"Sure, if you promise to not kick my ass too bad."

"Ha ha. No promises."

My eyes scan the door at the front of the line, and . . . yes! She's opening it. Art day! I love art day! We get to transfer what we made onto a brand new T-shirt, keep it, and wear it around wherever and whenever we want.

It's gonna look great. My colored rocket ship with its beautiful triangle nose and a lance coming out the tip, the U-shaped steering wheel in front of the seat of the cockpit, its rectangular body, triangle-shaped main wings and smaller rear ones, and heart-shaped rings of fire from its tail are gonna be so awesome! And I love that each part of it is in a different bright color.

"Yes!" The door opens.

"Hi, class. Welcome." Ms. Shay's sweet voice reaches the back of the line as I look behind me. Everyone's paying attention. Her pretty smile is solid and not like anyone else's, especially for a teacher. There's almost a glow around her. Her head tilts to look down both sides of our line. "Good job everyone. Please come in, one at a time. Slow as she goes. Please, no pushing."

We all straighten up a bit more.

"Hello, John." She nods. "Hello, Amy. Hello, Arash." She brightens her smile at me in a way that John and Amy don't get. My eyes turn into mini suns—wide and bright. I smile. I could sing.

"Okay, class, as we briefly mentioned yesterday, today we'll be taking your finished drawings and putting them on brand-new T-shirts for each and every one of you."

I like watching every move Ms. Shay makes with her hands, lips, and entire body as she talks and moves in little bits. It's like nothing can go wrong when I'm around her.

"John, come on up."

Dude, John, you better get finished quick like. And, Amy, you too. You both better listen super good and understand exactly what Ms. Shay is saying about working that machine. Make your shirts and skedaddle so I can go.

They do. I watch every motion they make and listen to every word Ms. Shay says. My turn.

"Arash, please step over here." Ms. Shay points to the floor in front of the big tan metal machine.

Yes!

"One more time, class. Now, everyone, please pay close attention. Watch and listen as I help Arash with his T-shirt, and then we're going to go a little faster as everyone understands." She looks at me like she could melt a mountain. "Arash, please take one of those T-shirts on the stack."

I hold the left sleeve and the left waist up horizontal and perfect. "Very good." Her bright brown eyes look at mine, and it's like she just put me in the softest, warmest prison that I never wanna escape from. She dips her head and whispers, "Nice rocket drawing, by the way. Love the different colors."

Now, I'm going to explode. My cheeks turn into two hot flames.

She puts her hands over mine and we hold the shirt horizontally, showing the class.

Oh, goodness.

"Okay, class, grabbing the shirt like this, you want to make sure you're laying the fabric flat on the cloth surface of the machine, front side up. Arash, check that it's flat, please."

Carefully, I check that it's perfect. "It's flat."

"Very good. Now take your drawing and place it picture side down onto the T-shirt and see if you can line it up square in the center."

I do, and I'm crazy amazed at how patient she is. And how nice. Definitely not normal.

"And now, I'll double-check." She lays her pretty fingers gently over my drawing and raises it slightly from where I had it.

Ah, she's right. It was a bit low for how tall the shirt is.

She lowers the submarine top of the machine on my drawing and shirt. "Now go ahead and press the red button."

Hsssss. Fsssss.

"Now we wanna wait about twenty seconds before we lift the top to make sure the picture has good adhesion to the fabric." She lifts it, takes out my shirt, and holds it by the shoulders for everyone to see. "Now we let it cool for a few seconds to room temperature." She smiles at me again. "Okay, Arash, moment of truth. Peel off the paper."

"Holy cow! That's awesome!" I surprise everyone with how loud I am. I pull my fist down by my side fast and strong. "Yes!"

Ms. Shay laughs. The kids next in line smile at me. "Yes, it is very nice. And I like how the rocket ship is horizontal across the chest of the shirt." She looks at me. "Well done." After a moment, she lifts her eyes to the next student.

"Thanks, Ms. Shay. And thank you for your help."

She looks back at me and winks.

I step aside, hold out my T-shirt, and stare at it. I turn one way and then another, looking at the perfection. Nothing's wrong. My eyes jump back to Ms. Shay, making sure she doesn't see me. I smile at my shirt. Can't wait to wear this awesomeness!

I fly home.

Knock, knock, knock! Come on, Dad. Come on! You have to open this door fast, dude. Let's go. I'm about to bust through it like the Juggernaut. I made this thing and you're gonna love it. Beautiful colors, amazing everything. Dude, open this freakin' door. I glue my ear to it. It's dead in there. But both their cars are here. Huh? I lean back and look again out the open front door: Toyota Supra, MR2, and the Camaro I saw in the driveway. Knock, knock, knock! It's the middle of the freaking day, and I know your ass ain't sleeping.

Suddenly, the door pulls open like a wild hurricane that almost sucks me in. "Fuck you want, man?"

"Hey, Pop! I made this. I want to show you! Look, Dad. Isn't it great?" I lift my shirt by its shoulders.

In a swoop faster than lightning, he snatches it! Everything suddenly turns to slow motion. The anger in his face and body explodes. He takes it in his hands, grabs it by the collar, and tears it clean down the front. He throws it back into my chest. "Is that what you wanted to show me?"

His eyes squeeze down as if to crush me. He disappears behind the door.

I can't move. Rocketship in my hands. Time stops.

Shelby appears as if out of a fog. Her scared brown eyes set themselves softly on me. "I'm so sorry, Arash." She tries to cover herself with her arms, pulling Dad's shirt across her and her naked legs. "We'll go out for ice cream later, I promise." She pauses and looks at me with eyes that half ask if she could go. She backs up slowly with her head down and closes the door.

Sex, huh? You tore it because I interrupted you. Okay then. Fuck you.

CHAPTER 13

He Won't Hear

"**A**rash, man! Fuck are you?"

A-hole. I'm not answering you. Go F yourself, and keep barking. Keep screaming. Watch how I won't answer.

"*Alo, kojayee baba.* Where are you, man?"

Farsi, shmarsi, I don't care in what language you say, "Hello, where are you?" and try to call me. But his voice is getting closer. Shoot. "In my room."

"Come, man. We are going now together for a drive, you and me. Come when you are ready to the front of the house!"

Eh, I don't wanna go nowhere with this guy. Looks like he's standing at the door.

"Ready, Son?" He looks me up, down, and away. He knows I'm pissed.

I meet him outside and look down the street. "You waiting for somebody?"

"What?"

"You were looking down the street." I can't look at him. I won't.

"No. Just thinking. That is not too important." He looks at the keys in his hand. "Let's go."

We pull into the 7-Eleven, and he clicks the ignition off. He looks straight through the windshield, then down at his thigh. "You want something from inside?"

"You mean *anything*?" My eyebrows jump up.

"Yes. Anything."

I squint at him for a second and wait for him to look back. He doesn't, but keeps his eyes on nothing.

"Sure."

We hop out, and I jump into the Sev. Before I know it, my fingers are getting cold sitting on the horizontal glass of the ice cream freezer. I look carefully through before sliding that bad boy open: Chipwich—not today, raspberry sherbet thing—ew, ice cream sandwich—meh, ice cream cones—taste like plastic. Oh, this is not even good enough. I slide the top glass and run my fingers under the main characters to see what else. No. No. Yes! Strawberry Shortcake ice cream bar on a stick. Jackpot! I'm already biting through those cakey, crumbly bits into the strawberry layer and the center creamy vanilla. I close my eyes and stay in heaven—not too sweet, not too strawberry—just perfect. "Hey, Dad, I need money." I wiggle the bar in my fingertips to show him.

His eyes come back to me, and he barely notices the ice cream. "Good, Son." He smiles.

"Mmm-hmm." Two bites, and half the bar is polished off before we hit the door and I wish I had a second one.

"Come, let's go to the car." Dad and I turn the corner.

For some reason, today seems different—calmer and gentler. As we step on the asphalt of the side lot, a warm breeze blows through, and it's like someone just calmed me and everything in the world. We get to the back of the Camaro, and suddenly, I stop.

"Hey, Dad?"

He stops, too, and turns to me.

"What happened to Mom?"

"What?"

"Mom, like my real mom. You know, back home. What happened to her? Why did we leave her?"

He turns immediately angry, like a stone that was just set on fire. He jets his neck into me like he's going to murder me. "What question are you asking now?" he says, with an assassin's eyes. His fists squeeze hard and match his angry face.

For some reason, I don't move a muscle. I'm not scared one single bit. "Mom—what happened?"

A volcano of lava is about to flow from the top of his head. Arash, you should back down, take it easy, cool down, and shut up. But nothing in me will do that. And nothing wants to. This is not going to turn into that belt beating I got, or any of the other ones. He's going to answer my question.

The veins on his neck want to tear free. His jaw muscles turn boulder-hard. "Now you listen to me, you little motherfucker. Your fucking mother is dead! She is dead! Do you hear me? Don't you fucking ask me about her again. She is finished! I am your fucking mother and your father! I am!" His screaming would normally tear holes through my ears and I'd get scared to death, or just start crying.

His face turns sharp like a spear and wants to go through me. All right, Arash, if you keep pushing, he'll want to beat you right here, but he's not going to answer. And if you go into the car, he's not going to answer there either. You're full of shit, Dad. You aren't my fucking mother. I look him straight in the eye and turn as hard as stone myself. I hate you for saying that, for not telling me the truth. I don't move, keeping my eyes locked on him.

Suddenly, he screams, "Get the fuck in the car!" He swings the door open, crashes into the seat, and slams the door.

Maybe I'll walk home. I look across the dirt field to our house, back at Dad, and at the empty passenger seat.

CHAPTER 14

Apology Split

Click. Snap! The sound of clanging metal rips through the hallway and into my room like a race car. I hate it when he opens his bedroom door like that. I should've closed mine.

I hear footsteps. Strangely, they're the quiet type. The speed and floor thumping isn't angry, and it isn't Dad's normal. They're slower and softer than usual. He stops at what sounds like just outside my door. He must be trying to see if I'm awake or if he can barge in. I whip the covers off, sit up, and listen close for what's coming next.

"Arash," he whispers.

You're going to need to give me more than that, Jake. I wait for his voice again.

"Arash," he whispers closer. His fingers slip through my cracked-open door and curl around the bare aluminum edge. I like that he's moving slow and not crazy. I watch his fingers like a hawk.

"Hey, Pop."

He slides the door, and his head peeks through. "Oh shoot, man. I did not realize you are awake. You were so quiet." His eyes catch mine, and he stretches a smile. "It's okay if I come in?"

Why is he asking, and why is he being so nice? It's like when he puts on the charm for people that he wants something from. "Yeah, come in."

He comes and stands right next to me.

"Shelby asleep?"

"You bet, man. She is still asleep. Fuck that shit—I am not going to wake her up." He shrugs and just stands there, looking a little goofy. "Can I sit with you, man?"

My stomach starts to squirm, and my shoulders squeeze together.

He sits next to me. "Listen, how are you?" His eyes are glued to me, but I can't look at him. It's like he's about to melt into me. "How you been? It's like, long time no talk, you and me."

Long time? Dude, it was just a few days ago that you wanted to murder me for asking about my mom. I wanna freakin' choke you. But your voice is so sweet now. "I'm okay." I look to the side.

"You know, I do wanna tell you that I heard what you said. I heard you asking about your mom. I did get hot, and I am sorry about that." He puts his arm around me, and his soft hand holds my shoulder.

I kind of want to cry, but the tears won't come. I wanna turn and hug him with everything I have, but I won't.

He turns his face away for a few seconds. "You know, I know you miss your mom." His throat grabs like he's going to cry. "I'm sorry about that." He gulps. Tears start, and his bottom lip turns down in that ugly way right before he gets loud about it. He wipes his eyes dry with the back of his hand.

I wanna be close. I so want to be close to you, Dad. I peek at him.

"Okay now," he starts. He puts his hand on my neck, holds it there, and squeezes gently. His hand is warm like heaven. He turns to give me the best half-smile he can. "I love you, Son." He bursts into tears.

"Love you too, Dad." My eyes fill up. His crying sounds go through my ears and come out my eyes. I don't want to cry too much. I want to let you cry, Dad.

He stands, eyes soft, whole body melting, and stops halfway out the door. He looks at the floor and in a crying voice, says, "We spend some time together soon, Son."

CHAPTER 15

A Forest Promise

"Jimmy! Get your ass out here!" I jump on his side fence and pull myself up so I can see the backyard. "You back there, Jimbo? Move it!" Maybe he's in his room.

Boom, boom, boom, boom! I slam on the front door. He's gotta be in his room messing with those freakin' Transformers. "Jimmy!"

He opens the door as calm as could be. "Hey, come in."

"Where were you? I was screaming all over the place."

"Just playing with Transformers and my turtle."

"No problem. Where'd your parents go?"

"Out to run errands. They knew you were coming over, so they were okay."

"Uh-huh." I look around his place. "Where's Shep?"

"He's probably out back digging holes."

"You get that tick problem fixed in the laundry room?"

"Nope."

"Dude, I ain't going in there. That freaks me out. It's like a zillion of 'em all over the walls and ceiling and everywhere. Blah!"

He smiles. "You want something to eat?"

"Let me guess, bologna sandwiches?"

"With mustard, don't forget." He pops his eyebrows up and down. "Let's get some pizza later."

"Now you're talking."

"Hey! I got a great idea! You want to go to that forest area near the other Sev, past the old-fogey home where we jump the speed bumps?"

"You mean that area where all the trees are?"

"Yes!" He lights up like someone lit his hair on fire. "Dude, you've never scouted there?"

"No. It's kinda weird over there."

"No, it's great! The most amazing forest and snakes and all kinds of cool stuff. I have to take you."

"All right. Hey, just don't pick up any dangerous ones. I know you like to do that crazy stuff. Is the pizza good?"

"It's fine. You know I know snakes." He shines his crazy eyes at me.

"Dude, just don't freak me out." I wonder if Jimmy ever notices that when we walk together, it's kind of peaceful.

"Mm-hmm."

I like to hear his yes even when he doesn't say it. "Whatcha think Robert is up to?"

"I don't know. He made me mad last time."

"What'd he do?" I look at his Transformers.

"He said some things about you I didn't like. He's trying to be my best friend. I told him you are. Then he said some more things about you I wasn't happy with. I'm not going back."

I like that. "He say bad things?"

"Yeah. No point taking the bikes since we're walking in. Let's just walk it."

"Cool."

We turn left off Fifth Street and cruise down Sixty-First Terrace.

"Ooh, is that what you're talking about?" I point four blocks ahead, where the street dead-ends, and just to the right.

"Yes, you can see the edge of it there—where those trees begin."

"You sure we can go in?"

He runs the back of his hand under his sniffling nose. "Mm-hmm. Done it before." He looks at me. He definitely wants to go.

"Not sure about this forest thing, dude." I shake my head a teeny bit.

"Almost there. Come on, this is gonna be amazing!" He runs across the street like he's never seen trees before.

"Wait up." We both slow down once we walk inside. "Wow, this place is interesting." The air is cool, tons of leaves and branches on the floor snap under our feet, and it's so thick of trees that only a little sun makes it from above. "It is pretty cool."

"See, I told you." He jumps and swings on a low branch.

"How many times you come here?"

"Few times. I scouted out this place a little." He looks at me like he's about to cause trouble.

But what kind of trouble can he cause here?

Jimmy bends down to pick up a bug.

"Don't give that thing to me, dude." I put my hand out as if to say "stop."

He smiles at the bug and puts it back down.

"Hey, Arash, just up here. Come check this out." He points straight ahead to the right. "Down there. Do you see it?"

"See what, dude? It's all the same stuff—trees and shit."

"Are you sure?" A sneaky smile flies off his face that says I'm missing something.

"What?"

"Up!" he points.

"Holy crap, is that a tree house?"

"Yup, and I've been in it, too. Let's climb the boards nailed to the tree."

"Sure they'll hold us?"

He races up like Spiderman.

I follow.

"Isn't it cool up here? It's dusty and old but still holding up." Jimmy scoots around, half bent over.

"Check it out. They even built a bench up here and a tiny table and chairs. The kids must have been young. We can barely stand up in this thing."

"Yeah, but if you sit on the floor, it's fine. Nobody's been in here for a while. It's like our own little world."

I smile back at him. I love to see him happy. I start cruising back down, and he follows.

"Hey, I wanna show you the barn. It's huge, and there's all kinds of horse stuff there, like giant needles and a bunch of crazy stuff."

"What?"

"Yeah, dude. Just through there where the trees end." We walk through. "There it is!" He points to the left, across the huge field.

"Is that a stable? It's giant. And what's that house on the right?"

"Never seen anyone there. Probably deserted. Come on. Let's go." We beeline to the barn.

"Stop right there, you kids!" a voice shouts from the house, scaring us both stiff.

My eyes dart to the man on the porch with something in his hand. "He's got a shotgun!"

Jimmy and I U-turn and bolt back into the trees.

"Holy shit, what was that!" Jimmy huffs.

We bend forward and hold our legs. We can barely breathe.

"Dude, that guy was freakin' nuts."

"Scared the shit out of me," Jimmy says.

We walk a bit, and time does that slowing-down thing that it does sometimes.

We're normal, and everything is happening normally; it just seems slower than normal.

Jimmy suddenly turns to me and stops. He stays quiet for a few seconds that seem like years. He's heavy and serious in a way I've never seen him. "Hey, Arash. I want to tell you—I want to promise you something. And I want you to promise me."

I freeze. What is this guy talking about?

"I want to promise you that I'll be at your wedding, and I want you to promise me that you'll be at mine." He just stands there, waiting to see that I heard him, and he won't move until I give him the right answer— our answer.

"Of course. Yes. Of course." What the heck? Anything for Jimmy, but what made him say that? And why now?

He takes a deep breath and smiles, and his shoulders drop like a thousand pounds fell off. He puts a hand on my shoulder and squeezes.

CHAPTER 16

Magic Shoes

"All right, team, today we're running the mile, as promised." Ms. Lacey looks at us.

I look up at the sky. It's one of those perfect mornings—like when a warm wind moves through cool air and calms everything. Reminds me of a good friend. It's gotta be a little past 11:00, but it's 6:00 a.m. quiet. Something about what Jimmy made me promise. Why did he say that? The clouds barely want to move, like they're waiting, or wanting something.

"Everyone form a line here." Ms. Lacey points to the track. "Don't worry—everyone will get a chance to go. You'll all line up in groups of four, with each group being a few feet behind the other. Be respectful. You can pass one another, but be aware of who's around you. I don't want accidents or to have to send anyone to the nurse's office today."

I'm not going to no nurse's office.

"Andy, George, Adam, and Lucy—first line." She walks them to their exact spot and points the tip of her cute, small foot to where she wants them to stand.

The sky is still so amazing.

"Ms. Lacey?" Fred raises his hand. "Can I go in the second line?"

"No, Mister—you stay where you are."

Poor Fred. His long, frizzy red hair hasn't seen a comb for a week—it flops and drags itself all around as he and his big-squared glasses back up into another kid.

"Ron, Catherine, Shelly, Arash—second line." We look up and walk to where she asks. I do like her. She's strong and clear. I watch every move she makes and every way that she makes it. Her top fits perfectly snugly and hugs her waist just right. Her shorts are mid-thigh—not too snug—and match perfectly. Everything seems just right about her, even her shoes. About thirty-five, I bet; that's what Dad would say, and he'd be right, nearly every time he talks to the ladies. Her black hair hangs straight just above the shoulders, and her fingernails are short—no polish—just the way I like. No makeup either, just a natural tan all over that glows. She's not Cathy pretty, but still cute.

"Arash."

My eyes snap to hers. "Yes." I stand ready at attention.

"Second line, hun."

I suddenly realize I never moved and start jogging to my position.

I watch the sky again. It's not fair that some days are this calm. It's like it doesn't matter what happens today, or ever, or who says what, how, or when; if the teacher says go or don't go, if this happens or that happens, what difference does it really make?

"Everyone ready?" Ms. Lacey shoots her pointer finger to the sky.

I bend forward and put my hands on my thighs. My brand-new navy Pumas with the Velcro straps that Dad bought are freaking awesome. So light and so snug. They hold my feet, ready to go with no complaining.

"Okay, now remember, four laps around. I'll call the count. Ready? Aaand . . . go!"

We're off, and the gravel track under my feet seems so easy. My legs lift light and fast, and I'm barely breathing. I pick up speed and move past Lucy, George, Adam, and Andy. I pick up more speed. I just flew by those guys like nothing. It's like even the wind can't catch me and everyone is standing still.

Halfway around the second lap, and I'm half a lap ahead of everyone and can't stop smiling. This is so much fun. My legs and feet keep going, like someone else is under them, lifting and lifting.

I cross the finish, and Ms. Lacey has her hand high up in the air. I stop and look out at the rest of the pack. Three-quarters of a lap behind.

"Nice job, Arash. Pretty fast." Ms. Lacey smiles softer than she usually does, but she's still tough. Always tough.

I shrug and lift my eyebrows like I don't know what the hell I'm doing. I don't. Everyone starts coming in. They look like they're from a different planet. Where did these people come from? Everyone's huffin' and puffin', some super hard, and some about to fall over.

"Arash, Arash!" Ron screams, throwing his hand up at me as he jogs.

"Dude, you're about to faint. Breathe."

"Stop everything, dude. I don't know where you went." He stops, bends over, and tries to catch his breath. "I don't know what happened. You just flew. I tried to catch up, but I couldn't. I can't breathe."

"I can see that, dude." I pat him on the back and look around. "It'll be all right."

CHAPTER 17

Not Today

Ding, ding, ding. Blip, blip. Weeshew, weeshew. Come on, you Asteroids freaking thing. "Don't die on me now. Go, go, go, go. No!" Shoot, I hate it when I explode. Set the game down on the shelf, Arash. Time for something more serious.

Opening the side door wide reminds me of the thinnest strip of side yard a kid ever did have. And the grass is still soggy from the rain. The frogs didn't jump all over my windows and croak crazy through the night. Must have not been heavy.

Bam! I jump horizontally on my bed. Never did a ceiling look so boring. Call up Jimmy? Nah. Walk around? Nuh-uh. Throw Chinese stars at our wooden fence and chase them into the neighbor's yard after they go through the slits? Hmm.

"Hey, Son." Dad slides the door open.

"Hey, Pop."

"I just need something, and then I go."

"Okay."

He moves quickly here and there. "You seen the scissors? You know, the small ones for the fingernails I hang on the nail here." He points to the spot above his bed, where the nail and the scissors on them usually are.

Uh oh, did I put them back? Did he take them? Shoot. "Uh, no. I don't think so." I keep staring at the blank ceiling, hoping he won't push.

"They are supposed to be here on the nail in the wall." He points again while giving me the death stare.

I hop off and jump over to look, pretending to care more than I do. "Don't think I moved them, Pop."

"Did you take the scissors, man? And you forgot?" His eyes tighten like they're going to cut me all over. "Because I put that shit back. You know I put that shit back on that nail right here because that is what the nail is there for, and I put it back. Now did you take it? I need to cut my fucking nails. And if so, find it. Now."

I don't know. I can't remember. My heart is pounding. I don't want to get hit—not for this. "I'll look." I jump all around, looking everywhere fast, and trying to look busy. Maybe I can buy some time.

"Here's the fucking thing, man. Now I am starting to get hot. You have two minutes to go and find those fucking nail scissors!" His lips squash together and his jaw muscles pop in and out.

I'm screwed. On the dresser and in it, my bed and the floor around it, on one of the wire closet shelves near the side door. "I'm looking, Dad. I'm looking."

"Okay, man, your fucking two minutes is up. Come here. I want to talk to you." His shoulders start to pull back and he wants me to stand in front of him.

Freak, somebody help me. Jeez, anyone. Please.

"Now you lost those fucking scissors. Did you hear me when I said to you to put things back in their place? Did I tell you, or did I not?"

My eyes check everywhere at lightning speed. Maybe God will make them appear any second.

"Look at me when I fucking talk to you!"

My ears start ringing. I look up at him.

"Now I fucking told you and you did not listen to me. What does that mean? That means you do not respect me." He starts looking like steam is literally going to shoot out of his ears. Like lightning, his hand swings.

My arm throws itself up to an outside block, crashing into his and stopping inches from slapping the living shit out of my face.

His whole everything turns to red, hot iron.

Our eyes lock.

He half wants to kill me and half doesn't know what to do with me.

"Don't you fucking block me!" He lowers his hand and stares me down, jetting his face forward like a suffocating blanket over me.

Something inside of me hardens. I'm not going anywhere.

He looks me down, then up again, huffs his nostrils, and storms out.

CHAPTER 18

Angel One

"Hey, Rico."

"Hey, Arash." Rico's strong eyes catch me. His straight black hair hangs shiny on all sides and barely covers the tops of his eyes. "Ride today?"

"Every day."

I sit next to him on the main walkway floor, our backs against the front wall of the school. Above our heads, in big black letters, reads: "Margate Middle School."

"You walk?" I ask him.

"Every day." He smiles and lifts his eyebrows in that smart-ass, harmless way I don't ever mind.

"Little shit."

"Ha ha ha," we laugh.

"Dude, is it crazy that it's already two weeks since middle school started?" Rico asks.

"I can't believe it. Honestly, I didn't see you the first day. How was it?"

I look around and down to my right. "Okay . . . I don't most tell people this, but I was a little freaked out." My voice gets low.

His eyebrows pop up. "How come?"

"I don't know, man. Maybe it's because we moved around so much and I changed schools so much. First, we lived in New York, then Maryland, and now here."

"That's a lot of schools."

"Yeah." I point to the sidewalk about fifty feet to our right, where all the bikes are plowing through each other to get to school. "Dude, I remember coming down that sidewalk, right there, and stopping. Right where the corner of the bike rack fence stops, I took my feet off the pedals, looked at the sign above us, and I was, like, crazy scared. I didn't want to come in. A few people behind me crashed into my back tire, I was so out of it." I look away, hoping he won't say anything mean.

"And how you doin' now?"

"I'm better." I look at his gentle eyes. "Thanks, dude."

He smiles and whacks me on the shoulder. "I like to come to school early and sit here. It's quiet, and I like to watch the people come in."

Another car stops at the drop-off driveway, two feet in front of us, and Rico watches.

"Who lives at home with you?" I pick up a pebble.

"Mom and sister."

"Oh yeah? How old is your sister?"

"She's eight. We're three years apart."

"That's cool. She seems nice by the way you talk about her."

"She is. I watch out for her and my mom. How about you?"

"My sister is four and a half years older. Dude, she is in her own world—half the time she's out doing God knows what. I wish we hung out more. You know, she's a teenager, everyone says."

"Yeah."

"Your mom doing good?"

"Uh-huh, she's usually busy with the house and making us food and stuff. She's good. You know, pretty busy." He looks down and around. Suddenly, he pops alive. "Hey, you need homework today?" His eyes go bright, and he whacks his hands on his backpack, ready to unzip.

"Dude, thank you so much." I grab his shoulder and smile. "Bro, by some miracle, I got all that shit done yesterday. I can't freakin' believe it myself."

"That's great, dude. Good for you." He nods.

"Hey! You wanna sit at lunch today?" He pops back up again.

"Yeah, dude. Of course."

"Awesome."

We look around, watching the last of the bikes pour in and get locked up. The bike area fence is huge and tall. They do steal a lot of bikes around here, that's for sure. The last-minute kids are being dropped off and racing not to be late, with their heavy backpacks bouncing up and down like they're going to crush the kid into the floor with each step. The bell is about to ring.

Rrrrrng. Rrrrrng.

"It's time." Ricardo stands, slips his backpack on, and hops while at the same time pulling the front of his shirt down from where the shoulder straps bunch it up.

CHAPTER 19

A Brother's Love

The sky is dark blue. Leaning against the front of this house, early morning, is the prettiest thing. The air, the trees, the cars—so quiet. Everything and everybody is peaceful. It's awesome. Nobody screaming. Nobody's mad, sad, or fighting. Just asleep. And no dad to hassle me.

"Squeak. Squeak, squeak, squeak. Squeak, squeak."

My eyes hunt the sound down to Dad's Camaro parked in 6142's driveway. It's so close. Could it be coming from there? I think I'm sure.

"Squeak, squeak, squeak."

Yup, I'm sure. Hard to see through this dim morning light though. Suddenly, something moves on the other side of the car, across the back part of the passenger window. Is that a head? It zigzags. More squeaking.

What the freak? Somebody trying to steal it? My heart starts racing. But why would they be crouched down? I walk to the front of the car and curve my head slowly around the side. Looks like a shadow of Howard's head wiggle. Body shape seems like him too. "Howard, psst, that you?" I wait a few seconds. "Howard?" The head turns to me.

"Hello."

I walk toward his familiar voice and start to make out that little-bit-wavy, semi-oily, parted-down-the-middle, blonde-brown mop of hair that bounces so funny. His head wiggles more just before I get close.

"Hey there, good buddy. What you doing up this gosh dong early?"

"Dunno. Just woke up." His eyes are glassy, like Dad taught me to watch for. Howard, tell me you're not drunk. I try to put on a happy face, but my stomach crunches.

He looks me up and down, nods in slow motion, and with more goofiness says, "Is Heecup awake?"

"No." I chuckle. "I think he's dead asleep. I hope. You know you have to stop calling him that." I hope he keeps that drunk laugh low.

"Who can say Yagoob, anyway? Sounds to me like Heecup. And it's got a good ring to it too. So Heecup it is." He nods to himself.

"I know it's hard to say Yaghoub. It's got a glottal stop, like the sound the back of your throat makes when you gulp."

Gulping and gulping again, Howard moves his head like a chicken.

"Ha ha ha. Yeah, but you can't keep saying Heecup. One of these days, you'll say it to him, and he's gonna open a can of whoop ass on you for that stupid shit. Just say Jake. Everyone else does." My eyebrows pop.

He stares at me with his eyes drunk open and tilts his forehead low. "Fine. In front of him, Jake, but with you, Heecup. Ha ha ha."

"What are you doing?"

He waves me closer. "First, I clean this here part of the paint."

"That was the squeak I heard."

"Uh-huh." He picks up a metal tub from the floor and takes its top off.

"Now, I'm gonna show you how to wax a car. Pay attention, little buddy—this is important."

"Hold on. Fuck you doing crouched down here waxing this car at like 5:30 in the morning?"

"Well, you know, amigo." Howard wiggle-grins, keeps his eyes half closed, and holds up his tub like it's a trophy. "I felt like coming out here and waxing me this here car, nice and purty." He nods with his eyes closed.

I roll my eyes so he can't see.

"Ever waxed one?" He stares right into the paint.

"Nuh-uh."

"Well, now, see here. You grab the foam thingy right on top of the wax tub. Then you rub it in little circles into the wax. Not too much pressure, just till you get you a nice but thin layer on your foam."

"But you can't see how much wax you're getting on it. Too dark out." I point around.

Howard looks at me like I'm nuts. "Never you mind that. Now look here. You know how long I been waxin' cars?" He slow-motion turns his head and barely gets his eyes open enough to look at me. "Like I was sayin'. Then, after you clean the paint or wash the car, you start puttin' it on in small circles, then bigger, till you got you decent sized circles. Like this." He rubs.

For being as drunk as he is, he sure is super precise with the way he's doing this. Like a foggy laser. Don't think he slept. He must have drank all through the night.

He pulls his head back a bit and tries to catch some of the barely blue light as the sky thinks about opening itself. "Now, see, after you put you on a thin layer, you have to wait for the wax to dry." He waves his fingers over the paint without touching it as if he's showing some super-gentle thing. "You have to watch it close now. You can't wipe it off too soon, or you ruin the whole thing. It's gotta be dried just right. How do we know it's ready? It starts to haze."

"Of course. But how do you see the haze? I can barely see you."

"You's gonna be a smart ass the whole day? Looky here from all angles, and you'll see enough. Now, if you think it's dry, you take a finger and rub gentle across, and if the wax comes off clean, you know it's right. No smudges. Now, if it's wet, even if you's blind you can tell it clumpin' under your finger as you pull, meanin' it was still wet." He puts the foam pad back on top of the wax tub, snaps the cloth off his shoulder, and wipes what he said was hazed. "You buff off like so. Then run your finger one more time, little buddy: ah, smooth as a baby's bottom." He smiles softly as his eyes close about three-quarters way. "And if water gets on it and you done it right, it'll just bead right off on account of the wax givin' you a layer of slippery protection." He sits on the driveway, takes a breath, and closes his eyes. After a few seconds, he looks at the sky, the paint, and then as if through the car and into nowhere.

I sit back and look at the sky too—so big and so forever. So pretty. It wants to lighten more, but slowly.

Howard pulls his knees to his chest and wraps his arms around them. He's quiet. He wiggles. "Did I ever tell you about my brother?"

I look and see him turned to me, looking at me with his far-away hazel eyes. He takes out an old picture from his wallet.

"That's him. That's my brother," he points, and with the softest eyes, Howard looks deep into his brother. "See how tall he is? Strong too. He's a few years younger than me."

I look close. Howard's brother is leaning on Howard's shoulder. I make out the big smiles on both of them and how close they seem. I turn to Howard. His eyes want to cry. But there's enough alcohol in there to stop it.

He hands me the picture.

"Is that your boat you guys are standing in front of?"

"Yeah, that's the one we'd go fishin' in, out in Radford. Everybody says Radford is ten years behind everyone—sayin' we're in the sticks and all. They're right, but I didn't mind it none. We'd love to go fishin'— Johnny 'specially loved it. Look how happy he is, how strong his face is.

Good lookin' guy too. Takes after his big brother, ha ha ha." He smiles that delayed smile I know while turning to the side. "Yes sir, but not as good lookin' as your brother there, Johnny boy." Howard melts into Johnny's picture.

Uh, should I let him cry? Should I say something? I don't even know what to do.

"We used to wax cars together, too. We'd love makin' 'em shiny and new—slick and smooth. We used to wax the windshield so rain would fly right off. He liked that."

I hand the picture back. "And he died?"

"He hung hisself. Over a girl. Yeah, he got real depressed—did it on a tree nearby the house."

Suddenly I can't breathe. I want to crush into a tiny ball and disappear. My head starts hurting. Oh God, I wish I could take all his pain and put it so far away that he'd never even see it, that he'd never know about it.

Howard goes stone quiet. Time starts to slow down, and the arms of forever want to creep around us.

Neither of us say or do anything. We just sit.

Bam!

We pop our heads up.

"Hey, you! Get back here, you bitch!"

"That's Dad's voice," I whisper to Howard.

"I think Shelby plumb broke your front door, she opened it so hard," Howard whispers back. His eyes bug out, and his neck goes straight. We don't move—our heads glued to the Camaro's passenger-side window so we can try to see through to the front yard on the other side.

"Why the fuck did you take off, man! You know, we were just talking, and suddenly you get up and storm the fuck out? What the fuck! You think you can do that shit to me?" Dad is volcano hot, and he's about to lava destroy her.

"Psst, Howard, he's going to freaking rip her head off."

"That Heecup is all fired up again, that's for sure." Howard turns to me slowly and with even slower eyes, turns his back to the car and slides down it, sitting again. "That Heecup will never learn."

"Keep it down, dude. I don't want him to hear you. He'll come over here, and then we're gonna get it too."

Suddenly, Shelby turns, stands right in front of him, and puts her face into his. "Listen, you motherfucker! You made me a promise, and now you're backing out. Fuck that! I want what I was promised, and you're going to give it to me. No backing out of nothing, you old, bald fuck!"

I whack Howard's arm.

"Ow! Hey there, little buddy. Don't be beatin' on your big brother now, ha ha." His head wiggles side to side, and he turns to peek through the window.

I want to jump up and beg Dad not to beat her. But I can't, 'cause maybe I'll get beaten and he'll still beat her.

The sky lightens up.

Dad leans into Shelby's face the way you don't want. "Listen, you fuckin' bitch. I ain't giving you shit. Who the fuck do you think you are, talkin' to me like that? Nobody talks to Jake like that. You fucking asshole! Don't you talk to me that way again, man, or I will fuck you up! I will kill you!" His fists pull back, like right before he hits someone.

"You go ahead, you fucking asshole! Kill me! Kill me now so the whole world can see. Being fucking dead is better than being with you. And then they'll ship your ass to jail where you fucking belong. Who gives a shit? I don't have anything. And all you do is fucking let me down."

Dad pauses. He never pauses. Suddenly, his eyes get huge and lava is about to bust out of the top of his head. Oh shoot—no stopping him now. I want to close my eyes, but what about Shelby? Dad's arm suddenly bends at the elbow and cocks back. Back down, Shelby—please—just back down.

Shelby suddenly bursts into tears and covers her face. But nothing can stop her loud-as-hell sounds as they rip through the Camaro and into my guts.

Dad gets immediately confused. His fists drop. His eyes start moving around Shelby's fingers to see what exactly is happening with those tears. She can't stop crying. Those deep hollow inhale sounds say it's real. Dad bends his head in all directions around her to get some clue of what to do. A second ago he was a raging I'm-gonna-take-a-swing-at-her maniac, and now he's softer than most guys. Even his salt-and-pepper, curly hair that dangles from the back looks soft and confused.

"Shelby? Are you okay?" Dad keeps trying to see her eyes. He moves to touch her arm.

But before he can, she cries another hellishly loud one.

"I'm . . . I'm sorry about that, Shelby. You know, sweetheart, sometimes I get hot, and I do apologize about that. I know I did say I will give you a house—something of your own, so you know you can stay there peacefully and all that. Don't worry about nothing now. You don't need to cry. It's okay. Come here now. Everything is all right." Dad brings her into his arms, but her crying just gets louder as her chest pulls in and out.

She breaks away.

CHAPTER 20

The Last Straw

"**A**h!" A huge breath rushes into me as I sit on my bed and look around. My insides are jumping all over the place. The clock says it's afternoon, and the sunlight outside agrees. I lie back down, and my heart has a second to fall back into place. Must've passed out in the car. Dad must've put me in my bed. Strange. I can't remember. Arash, don't worry. Just relax here for a few minutes.

"Get the fuck out of this house! Get the fuck out now! I don't want to see your face ever again! Go now!" Dad's scream blasts through the hallway and into my room.

I freeze.

"Stop telling me what the fuck to do and when to do it! Fuck you! You can't tell me who I can see and when! I'm gonna get the fuck out of this house! You can threaten me, you can beat me, but I'm getting the fuck out, you asshole!" Orly's voice blasts back, super strong and fiery.

God, I hope he doesn't make her shut up. I want to go out there, but I don't. I want to help her, but if I do go, Dad will go crazy just seeing me and maybe hurt her more. I can't let that happen. I want to help him, too, but I can't even get close. If he wanted to beat her, he would have done it already. Sounds like they're just going to scream today, apparently for a long time. I have to get up and see. I sit up, and my left foot touches the floor. "Ow!" An electric shock runs right through it. I limp to my door. I don't want him to see or hear me. His crazy inside might explode for no reason. Ghost-like, I stick my face against the curtain-covered edge of the door. I drift an eyeball sideways to peek through the open sliver. He's just a few feet away with his back to me. He looks like he's about to tear her in two. Orly faces him, straight on. What's he furious over? What did she do now? He's always picking on her, and I don't like it. I can't even listen anymore—the same repeating back and forth. They go nowhere. I don't think she'll talk to me about what's happening here.

"I don't want you to see those fucking friends of yours! Do you hear me? They are a fucking bad influence—smoking and drinking and party-ing all fuckin' night. You should not be hanging out with those nobodies!"

"Fuck you! You're never around—you don't give a shit—what do you care who I hang out with? You can go fuck yourself."

Holy crap! I could never say that to him. Freak. She's got some nuts. But she might get beaten. I pull my head back from the door. You have two choices, Arash. Go into your bed, pull the covers up over your nose, and pretend to be asleep. For sure, he'll leave you alone then. Or you can just sit here on your bed and wait for the disaster to clear up before heading out. Shoot, there's a chance he'll storm in here just for the heck of it and attack me. I can't lie down.

A couple of minutes pass that seem like years, and not a word. I don't get any hint of crazy stuff. My eyes squint, and my ears turn into listening needles, and they zoom through the house. I wish I could become one with the walls and carpet out there to know exactly what is going on with them.

I peek into the hallway. It's clear. I see the beautiful sunshine through the open front door. Be careful, Arash. Not yet. Nice and slow. Deep breath. I hope, hope, hope that his doors aren't open. I don't want to be nabbed and my life squeeze-squashed.

I start walking out, slow and steady, down the hallway. A few more steps and I'll be clear. The floor just barely creaks under me. I stop before his door. It's cracked a few inches, but enough to slide by. I shouldn't; I'm probably gonna get busted. If he stops me, he might send me back to my room, or even worse: have me sit down next to him and ask me a bunch of stupid freaking questions I have no idea about. Why Orly is the way she is? What is she doing? Who is she with? Blah, blah, blah. I'll have to be quiet and let him blabber on. Please, oh please, if there is a God, let Dad not call me and stick me in the jail of his endless questions. Just across his door . . .

"Arash!"

My guts drop into my legs, my cheeks go red hot, and I freeze.

"I know you're there. Come in, man!" His voice is angry and holding back in a way I don't like.

I take a breath, stand a little taller, and walk in. He's sitting on his floor mattress, death-staring me before I even walk in. I look at him, trying to keep a stone face and not show anything, especially fear. I don't think he's sure yet that I'm afraid. Otherwise, he'd already have crushed me with his yells. Hold it together.

"Come sit with your father now." His face and whole body are hard like iron. His hand starts tapping the mattress on his side.

I gulp. It's gonna be a long talk all right—heavy as the *Titanic*, and one I don't want to hear, but I'm gonna have to. Here we go. I keep my head down. He's staring at me from the side, probably with rifle eyes that could kill a horse.

"You heard that commotion, Son? You were in your room, close by? You were listening?" He waits calmly for me to answer right.

I lift my head just enough to peek at him from the corner of my eye and make sure he sees it.

His head turns more toward me, and his lips press together. He knows the truth and will beat me if I don't say it exactly right.

"Yeah, I was there. I heard." I turn my eyes from him and back to the carpet in front of me.

"Why didn't you come out? What did you do in your room? You were afraid?"

Now he's deciding what he's going to do with me. My shoulders pop up and my eyes tuck further down. "I stayed in my room. I was scared." Somehow, I'm not half as afraid as I thought I was going to be.

He pauses for a few seconds.

I look at him, and his eyes drift over the floor and away from me, not totally happy with my answer. Maybe he was expecting me to lie and that he would get angry with me.

His stare is ax-like, sharp—even the air in the room moves when his eyes cut through it. He nods and keeps his lips squeezed together. "Okay. You can go." He looks away from me.

What! "Hallelujah!" flashes inside me and in the whole room. Somebody just rang a church bell. I can go. Keep your face stone cold, Arash. Dad is very serious now. My insides are dancing. I get up slowly, making sure not to make any moves that would pull me back into problem land. I'm going in a thousand different happy directions as I start walking out slowly. My shoulders drop.

CHAPTER 21

Ring, Ring

"I called her today." Orly looks at me with the weight of a thousand dump trucks on her eyelids and shoulders.

My eyes pop open. "Called who?"

"Mom." Orly looks at me like I should know, squinting her eyes a tiny bit.

Oh shoot, she's talking about Mom. "What?" My eyebrows jump, my head moves back, and I rub my head.

"I can't stand this shit anymore. These fucking people. I can't stand his face, and I can't stand her. I gotta get outta here, Arash!" She looks up and away, disgusted.

I look her over: her crossed arms, the one leg with the foot turned out to the side when she's standing and doesn't care, and everything about her that says she's dead serious. Is she really going? Is she done?

Oh my God. What's gonna happen? A million questions race everywhere at once. Where's she going to go? What's gonna happen to the family? To me and her? It's like I'm going to explode this instant into a million stars and spread all over the sky. Hold it together. "Wait a second. What did Shelby say? What did you say?"

"I got so fed up after the millionth time he and I got into a fight. And Shelby—always taking his side. That motherfucker is never there. He doesn't give a shit about me." Her eyes start to tear. "But I told Mom— our real mom—that I can't stand this fucking place! I told her she has no choice and that she has to fucking get out here and get me. I don't care why she hasn't been able to come or what shit she's doing or what's going on. She needs to come and fucking get me, and that's it! I told her I need her to and that I *will* get the fuck out of here. She said she's going to come. I said she better because it needs to happen and I'm getting the fuck out—one way or another. She got the message."

My throat grabs. I can't speak. Is this for real? Is my sister for real? It's like someone is pouring molten lead on my head and everything is slowing to a stop.

"You know..." She looks at me—her eyes are tough, honest, and know how to go deep into me. "You could come. It's only a matter of time before it gets bad for you. This is no place for you—for either one of us. I know you love Dad, but if you decide to come, then come. You'll be safe. You'll be with me and Mom."

My head goes blank. Everything turns a yellowish-white. My throat wants to cry. Me? Go where? I can't go anywhere. I love my dad. I can't leave him. I won't.

CHAPTER 22

Breakfast Hearts

Honk, honk!

"Yes! Sunday breakfasts are the best, doo da, do da," I sing as I walk out the door. "Hey, Jimmy! I'm coming! Hang on."

Jimmy sticks his head out the car window. "Hey, Arash! Come on!"

I run for the Bronco and hop in. "Hi, Mel. Hey, Linda. Nice to see you both." I hit Jimmy with a good handshake.

"Hey, Arash." Linda looks back.

Always nice to see her.

"Hi, Arash." Mel looks at me through the rearview. "So you ready for some breakfast? Bring your appetite?" Is he smiling or not? I can never tell.

I don't want to be too excited. I mean, he's paying, but I don't want to not be excited either. "Yes, Mel. Thank you. I'm ready for a good breakfast. And thank you both for having me." I hope that's good.

Linda throws her hand in the air. "Oh, Arash, you know we love to have you. It's our pleasure." She whips her head around and sparkles her eyes at me.

Jeez, it's pretty when she smiles—like the sun is in there, beaming out everywhere.

I catch her eyes and my chest goes funny.

"Hey, Jimmy, what's up? Good to see you."

"Good to see you too." He lifts his chin at me with a devious smile. I do the same.

We laugh. We're gonna cause some trouble today, or we'll want to.

"Everything cool with you?"

"Yeah, everything's good. Hey, Mom and Dad said that they might drop us off at my house to hang out after. You cool with that?"

"Kidding me? Sounds amazing."

"Dude, it's like crazy hot today. We should see if we can toss eggs up, super high, and see if they'll cook on the blazing asphalt. We should do it on my street, right in front of my house. I've heard of people doing it. His eyes go big, like two crazy spheres of cold ice."

"Sweet!" Jimmy the troublemaker. "I love it."

"Okay, guys, we're here."

"Arash, let's go!" Jimmy races out.

"Coming!" I jump out.

We hang out at the entrance for his parents and open the door for them.

"Hey, Arash, what do you think you'll get today?" Mel says as he looks at me, then back down at his menu.

Whoa, Mel is talking to me. That's pretty cool. He's so quiet, and usually I can't tell if he's angry or just quiet. So nice to see him happy. "Um, maybe the french toast."

"That's a good call. Can't go wrong with that." He lifts his glasses off his nose and smiles a small one. "Think I'll go for the Dutch baby." He looks at Linda. "Hun, how about you?"

"Mmh, not sure." Linda keeps looking.

Food, eat, and we're ready to jump out of our seats. Jimmy and I look at each other. I know what he's thinking, and he knows me.

"Dad, Mom, Arash and me are done. Can we go outside?"

Mel looks at Jimmy, me, and Linda. "Okay, you two, take off."

"But don't go too far, kiddos. I wanna be able to find you without having to track you down." Linda widens her eyes at us.

We look at each other.

"Okay, Linda, I'll make sure." I look at Jimbo.

We dart for the doors.

"It's nice out here. We have at least fifteen minutes before your parents are done."

"Dude, for sure. Wanna scout around?"

We start walking the parking lot, balancing on the concrete strips that surround the grassy patches, and jumping on whatever we can.

"Hey, Jimmy, your dad sure is in a good mood."

"Yeah, dude. I have no idea what's goin' on."

"Ha ha. You know he's so generous and nice—bringing me out with you guys for breakfast almost every weekend. I mean, not to mention also taking us boating, fishing, and all that stuff. He really does a lot."

Jimmy's whole body lightens up. Then he looks down and puts his hands in his pockets like he's thinking about his dad. "He likes the water and all that stuff. Also, my parents really like you."

"Thanks, dude."

"Also, I think sometimes they don't want me in their hair, bothering them, so they keep us busy with each other. But, hey! It's much better when we're together."

"For sure!"

We jump on and off the rocks nearby and spin in the air.

"Hey, uh, I need to tell you something. Something I hate."

"What's up?"

My parents told me a few days ago that . . . uh, we're leaving. We're gonna be moving."

"Moving! What? Dude, are you serious?" My brain starts spinning a million miles an hour, shooting electric sparks everywhere. I want to explode.

"They didn't tell me everything, but they usually don't tell me everything. Something about how the neighborhood is going south and they want more space, like out in the country."

"Dude, are you serious? When?"

"Couple of weeks. They said Jupiter, Florida—it's out in the country, about an hour away. Lots of space and land. There's a lake there too. I haven't seen it yet." He looks at me and jumps close. His eyes are sad and they're saying sorry. "I told them they're gonna have to bring me back to visit you. And that you have to come out too." He high-fives me with everything he's got.

You're moving? Holy crap. "Uh, yeah. For sure. Definitely, dude! I'm definitely coming out. And you come out here for sure."

CHAPTER 23

Seen, Unseen

"**H**ey, Arash."

"Hey, Ray."

Like two arrows meeting, he comes from the center courtyard toward me, and I walk along the back of the school, ending up side by side, both heading to our next class.

"How'd you like PE today?" The laces on his short, tan suede boots click-clack softly with each step.

"It was pretty cool. Fun."

"I can't believe the way you hit that ball. Dude, you hit it farther than the teacher. And that was really your first time swinging a golf club?"

"Never held one before. But after the golf coach came in and showed us all how—it was so natural and comfortable to hold the grip, like I'd held it for a hundred years. And then . . . I just swung at the freaking thing and it sailed. When it went past Coach Liz's shot, I kinda freaked out. I thought she'd be upset or even worse—embarrassed. But she was cool. And when the kids went, 'Ooh!' I thought, 'Yeah, pretty good shot.'"

"Pretty good is right. That was freaking cool." Ray looks at me with his eyebrows gently up.

"Thanks." It's like a balloon just inflated in my chest.

He passes his fingers through his straight reddish-brown hair and sweeps to the side; it pays no attention to him and falls back perfectly with just a few hairs staying over his one eye.

This guy is like otherworldly cool. I can't believe he's even walking with me. Talking with me and wanting to have a conversation—forget about it. Does that mean I'm awesome too? I don't understand how nothing seems to bother him. I get why all the girls like him. There's something gentle about him—something easy. But it's more than that. I can't quite figure it out.

"Hiii, Raaay." A super-cute girl beams glowing eyes at him as she walks by. Her and her friend giggle.

"Hey." Ray glances at her and looks away—no waiting, no trying to talk to her more, no nothin'. He is zero affected by the hotness that just came and went. How is this possible? I'd be squirming and trying to do everything for her. But not Ray—cool and unaffected one bit. It's as if nothing just happened.

I don't get it.

Our classes are coming up. We'll have to split. My tummy starts to go funny.

"Hey, Arash, you wanna meet up after school today? We could hang out. It'll be cool."

My eyes explode inside my head where no one can see. Keep it cool, Arash. Holy crap! "Yeah, that sounds good." I nod.

"How about the Del Taco across the street from school? We can get something to eat. Four thirty sound good?"

"Sounds great, dude. I'll be there."

"Cool. See you." He raises his hand as he turns to head to class and his eyes say a warm goodbye.

"Later." Holy crap! I can't think of anything. Teacher this, smeacher that. Algebra, English, who cares? I'm gonna meet up with Ray! I'm gonna be the coolest guy. Everybody is gonna love me! I'm gonna love me!

Race home, Arash. Tell Dad, drop your bag, drink some water, chill for a bit, and then jump back on the bike and head to Del Taco. Yes! But who's gonna be able to chill? Yoohoo!

I fly home, skid through the driveway, and stop.

Shoot, no cars. Not good. "Dad! Dad! Crap, freaking bike—get out of my way." I toss it down. "Dad! You home?" But he's not here. Maybe someone borrowed both his cars. Not a chance. He always keeps wheels nearby. He doesn't like to be stuck. I jump inside for a one-in-a-million possibility. Everything is dead silent. I go outside, look up and down the street, and try to listen around the corners of the streets.

After a forever amount of minutes, suddenly . . .

Rumm, rumm, errrr!

Dad turns fast into the driveway and stops even faster.

Yes! Everything's gonna be just fine. Plenty of time to get to Ray.

Smile, Arash. Get ready. "Hey, Pop. Hey, uh, guess what?"

He gets out of the car and turns to me. No expression.

"My buddy, Ray, one of the coolest guys in the whole school—okay, the girls love him. He's amazing. He wants to meet up with me at Del Taco—you know, the one across from school. I'll bike over there, I'll be back before dark, and I'll do all my homework. I promise."

He looks at me and says nothing.

It's like someone just threw a bomb at my feet.

"You can't go. Tae kwon do is tonight." He walks like his body just turned into ice and heads to the house.

"Dad, please." I want to beg. "I go to tae kwon do so much, almost every day. Please, this is really important. I wanna go."

"No! You're doing what I say. No more talk. Forget this guy. One more word and I'm gonna get hot." He goes to his room and shuts the door.

I wanna fall to my knees and pray to God. Dad can't do this.

CHAPTER 24

Love Scared

The way she leans against the wall—the backs of her shoulders rolling side to side as she laughs. Her best friend, Angela—Miss Beautiful in a Box—giggles next to her. The way the sun bounces off that wavy red hair as it stretches down her mid-back—yeah, I think I'm gonna melt now. This one is something else. I mean, there's hot, and there's smokin'. She crosses her legs in a way she likes and chews gum like the freest person in the world. Can't take my eyes off those legs that cruise up thigh-high where her shorts stop them. The skin on her neck is so soft when she turns to Angela, and I like to watch her jaw as they talk. It's kind of funny that she's almost a head taller than every girl in our class, but it doesn't change her any in my eyes.

"Hey, Arash. Whatcha doin' out here by yourself?"

"Harry, dude, you scared me. Where'd you come from?" I look at Debrah to make sure she didn't move.

"I just came from over there. Right off to the side. Are you okay?" He squints his eyes, looking me over.

"Uh, yeah . . . um, good. Just hanging out here, and then I was gonna over and see some of the guys. You know."

"Oh, cool. I just saw you standing by yourself and thought to say what's up. What did you think of the meatloaf today?" His eyebrows hop up and down at me.

"Uh, it was fine."

"Okay, that's like the best lunch of the week. Are you crazy? You sure you're okay?"

He's right. It was good.

He keeps staring at me, and I need him to go away. Come on, dude, beat it. I got a girl to stare at from across this playground.

"Okay, I guess I'll catch you later. Let's hang out at lunch sometime."

"Yeah, sure." I keep my eyes glued on the redhead as I run my hand through my hair.

"Cool!" Harry smiles and bounces off.

Start walking around, and stay as far away from her as possible while still keeping an eye on her so she doesn't move. But it's important she doesn't see you. It's important that she doesn't get a hint of what you're up to. Now, all you have to do is walk around, to the end of the playground, behind the corner of the wall she's standing on, bust a U-turn, walk back along the wall like you've always been there, and, voila, you run into her, Arash.

I come around the corner as if I got there naturally. She's still where she's supposed to be, and she's chewing gum beautifully. Thank God she hasn't moved. Angela is still talking and laughing. All is good. I take a deep breath, look up at the sky and then at the kids on the playground, and she's coming up fast. Yes! And no! Oh shoot, Arash, hold it together. Just a bit more. Suddenly Angela's head turns and her eyes lock on mine. I quickly look away and then back at her.

She giggles.

Gulp. Shoot! Debrah's eyes do the same, just as strong—maybe stronger, but somehow softer too. My eyes catch hers, and instead of being twenty feet away, it's like we're face-to-face. So this is what it's like to walk and be frozen at the same time. Hope no one else can tell.

Debrah raises her hand and wiggles her slim fingers at me. "Hi, Arash." She smiles as bright as sunshine and tilts her head to the side.

I'm gonna die now. "Hi, Debrah." I lift my hand and smile while I have my heart attack.

CHAPTER 25

Fly, Birdie

"**K**nock, knock." Hmm, no answer, but I hear a heck of a lot moving in there—rustling and all kinds of stuff. "Knock, knock." Come on, open the door.

Her hand grabs the doorknob on the other side. "Hey, Arash." She moves back to her bed, where an open suitcase sits a quarter filled with clothes. She darts, laser-focused, to her dresser to grab more, fits it in perfectly, and then shoots to another part of the room for other stuff.

I don't think I've ever seen her so focused, so sure of what she's doing.

She whizzes by me to the bathroom just outside her room and comes back just as fast.

"Whatcha doing?"

"Packing."

"Packing for what?"

She stops like a thunderbolt in her tracks and stands right in front of me.

My heart skips a beat and my throat catches. I breathe a little fast but hide it good.

Orly looks at me gently. "Mom's in California now, remember? I called her and told her to come get me?"

"Oh yeah." That's right. That thing.

"Well, she's there—she arrived a little bit ago. She found a place not too far from her sisters. She told me to come now. I have a ticket. I'm going like in . . . three days. Remember when I said you can come?"

Oh, shoot. But that's now? Three days? Everything goes blank.

She puts her hands on my shoulders and pulls me in for one of her famous long and deep hugs. She pulls away slowly, dips her head, and catches my eyes. It's like I can see forever in her eyes, and she sees the same in mine.

My eyes start to tear.

"Hey, hey. Don't worry. Come out to visit us. I would love that, okay?" She stays with me. "Okay?" She keeps her hands on my shoulders and won't let go until I answer.

"Okay." The tears start really running now. I pull her in for my hug.

I let her go, and she goes slowly back to packing. Everything about her shines brighter than I've ever seen. I hear what she's saying, but I don't want to. It's like everything is happening and I'm not here.

"Do you wanna hang out with me while I pack?"

"Okay."

"Just sit on the bed here. Tell me what you did today. How was school?"

I want to let the tears burst out all over the place. "It was okay, not much. Kinda dull. Oh! The other day—there's this girl at school. She's so pretty."

"Yeah?" Orly stops what she's doing and turns to look at me with that twinkle in her eye. "Tell me more." She brightens up, like five times usual.

"Well, I think she's the prettiest girl in the whole school, so I walked by her at lunch and she said hi. And I said hi back. It was amazing."

"That's awesome! Sounds like she likes you, little bro."

My throat catches. "You think so? I hope so."

"Let me tell you something." She kneels in front of me and takes my hands. "When we like a guy, we do that kind of stuff. We look at them, we play with our hair, we say 'hi' all cute. Trust me, she likes you. You should talk to her."

"You're probably right. What would I say?"

"Say anything." She goes back to organizing her clothes inside and outside the suitcase. "Talk about school stuff. Ask her about her friends. Ask what she likes to do after school and what her favorite things are."

"Sounds like a pretty good idea, I guess." Kinda sounds scary as all hell at the same time.

"See, your sis will help you out."

She sits next to me and hugs my shoulder into her.

CHAPTER 26

Love Returns

"Jimmy's coming today! Jimmy's coming! Yoo-hoo! Yes!" I dance and wave my arms.

"Arash! Is that you making commotion?"

"Yes, Dad! I'm singing and happy! Jimmy is coming!" I blast from my room.

"Okay now, singing is good! I thought you were doing some crazy shit or something, man. Okay now, no problem!" He shoots back. "By the way, you know I just heard some honking from outside—you should check on that."

"Yessss!" I lightning bolt to the open front door and straight through. "Jimmy!" I put my hand in the air. Mel and the Bronco are at the curb. "Jimmy!"

Jimmy rolls his back window down, leans in the center to his parents, opens his door, and bolts out.

"Hi, Arash!" Linda waves. "We'll come back for you guys in a couple of hours. Have fun, boys."

Mel's gentle eyes lock on mine. He waves.

"Hey, Arash!" Jimmy gives me a super handshake.

"What's up, Jimmy Jimbo? My favorite redheaded, freckled friend!" I pull my fist down hard and fast against my side. "Yes!"

"Ha ha ha." Jimmy laughs and nods.

"Dude! Whatcha got in your hand? Holly smokes, let me look at that remote-control car."

Jimmy hands her over.

"She's a beauty! Where the heck you get this thing?"

"Just got it—it's pretty sweet." He points at the decals on the white-bodied beauty with the flat nose and racing stripes.

I almost start to drool. "That's freakin' cool! I love it. Let's go in and get mine and we'll take them up the street."

"Man, I couldn't wait to get the fuck outta there."

"Your house?" I look back at him as we walk in.

"The car, dude. I was going crazy in there. I thought I was going to explode and kill somebody."

"Okay, let's just take it easy, dude. Long ride?"

"Sometimes I get frustrated. I'm so glad I'm here. I like it here, hanging with you."

"Come on, let's go to my room and get it."

I pick it up with two hands like it's a delicate trophy.

"Dude, that thing is sweet! Porsche? Never saw it before."

"It's the 935 Turbo Porsche. How freakin' cool is it?" It's like my hair is gonna burst into flames I'm so excited.

We walk up the street, toward Highway 441, and it's as quiet as ever between us, and just as peaceful.

"Jimbo, check out this awesomely newly paved parking lot over here! It's smooth as a baby's bottom—perfect for our cars. Let's put these babies down and see what they can do."

"Yes!" Jimmy puts his down, and it takes off like a rocket.

"Holy cow, yours is so freakin' fast! Mine is Mr. Slowpoke. You're running circles around me."

We laugh.

"I'm gonna have to get one of those."

We race 'em around, and he keeps smashing into the side of Mr. Porsche.

"Let's drive 'em over to the tree over there."

"More snakes Jimbo?" I look at him from the side.

"Shut up, dude. You know I love snakes. I want to climb."

"I would've never guessed." I jog after him.

Jimmy runs to the tree, jumps, plants one foot on the trunk, pushes off, grabs the lowest limb, and pulls himself up to sit on a branch.

"Show-off."

"Ha ha. Come up."

"I jump on a lower branch."

"What's going on with your pop, that Mr. Jake? Is he still getting himself in trouble with the police?"

"Dude! A few weeks ago the sheriff came by, asked everybody a bunch of questions, and then hauled off one of the tenants in 6140, handcuffs and all. My dad said the dude had cocaine in his room or something, but that he had nothing to do with it."

"Holy shit! What the fuck, dude? Cocaine?"

"Dude, they even took my dad to jail."

"What?" Jimmy's eyes pop open and out of his head.

"Dude, for real. Apparently the law says something about possession— like if there is cocaine on the property and it's the renter's, the landlord is responsible for it being there too. Something like that. It's always some shit around here. If guys aren't fighting each other with pipes and wrenches over a girl, or putting each other's head through the drywall, then it's cocaine and cops."

"Ha ha ha." We laugh out loud.

"That's some good action. We could use some of that in Jupiter, dude. It's quiet as fuck, like all the time. I love the space, but it gets so boring. Sometimes it's too quiet. Nothing to do and no girls. I'm dying."

"No girls? Yup, then I know you're dying, ha ha ha. I like the quiet sometimes."

"Yeah, I know you do." He looks at me with devilish eyes.

CHAPTER 27

Ear Shock

"**A**rash!" Dad calls from way off.

Freak. "Yeah, Pop! What is it?" I holler back.

"Come the fuck over here, man. I have something to tell you."

My insides sink. I already don't want to hear whatever it is he wants to say. Am I in trouble? I don't like his voice. Why am I so nervous? It's nothing, Arash, just relax. He probably just had a bad day. I walk into his room.

"We have something we want to tell you, now at the moment." He stands next to Stepmom, almost squirming.

Strange. He never looks afraid. Why am I scared?

"Look, man—you know how your mom has always wanted a house of her own." He stands close to Shelby, but not too close. He looks at her and turns to me in a way he's not comfortable with. "Well, we found her one not too far from here—up the road a little ways. You know where Lauderhill is, just near the Army Navy down 441. And I am sorry to tell you, man—you know this is not easy for me to say—but she will be living there from now on." He looks at her.

Shelby looks at him, at me, at the floor, and then slowly up and away.

My eyes squeeze and blink. There's that silence again. My ears hurt, like there's a needle in the center of each one pushing through.

"Okay, man." Dad wipes tears from his eyes after he missed the few that traveled down the crease of his cheek. "We should go now, and, you know, we can talk more later about this."

But there won't be a later. And there won't be any more talking. My legs are heavy, like they just got anchored through this shaggy carpet and won't budge an inch. I hate this dungeon of a place, the dim light, and everything about it.

Dad and Shelby bend their heads down and to the side. They just stand there, barely looking at me or each other.

CHAPTER 28

Sweets and Sales

"**A**rash! Are you home motherfucker? Ha ha. Where are you, Son? I got something to show you."

I hop off my bed, and I'm not going to say a word to you until I cruise down the hallway, where you'll see me in about five seconds.

"Hey, good to see you." He grabs me, squeezes me one-armed, and shakes me. "Look what I got you: Some of that bubblegum tape you like, a Charleston Chew–you know the ones you eat frozen when you go with your friends to the public pool in the summer–I know you love that shit. And also a Whatchamacallit–one of your favorites too." He lifts his head. His eyes are happy. He hands me the bag.

"Thanks." What's wrong with you? Something's off, but I can't tell what. The eyes and hug are softer than usual. Something's fishy all right.

"No problem, man. I thought you would like that. You know, we have to take care of each other and all that. That's how it goes."

What are you saying right now?

He heads for the side patio door to look at something outside it. He turns back. "You hungry, man? How about we go for pizza? Are you hungry for pizza?"

"Mmm, I could eat."

"Okay, man, let's go. You and me together."

"Where we going?"

"Coral Springs. Next to Master Jae's place. In the mall, they have that beautiful pizza place. I think I took you and Mom there. Okay, now, let's go." He starts walking to the car, almost not knowing where I am.

The Camaro passenger seat seems like it's the only one in the world today, off on some island, moving by itself. Who's going to have pizza? Why did he come into the house with gifts? And what kind of weird mood is this? It's like I'm in that scene from *The Twilight Zone* where the guy in the diner finds the magic pocket watch that stops time, clicks it repeatedly to stop and start everyone, leaves them stopped in time, and just watches them like that.

"What's going on? Everything cool?"

Now how do you want me to answer that, doof? I don't wanna move to no new house. I just don't wanna do it. "Everything's fine, Pop." I look out the window.

We pull into the mall.

"All right, we're here. Let's go."

"Di'Angelo's Pizza," reads the sign above the joint.

"Hello, sir. Young man. How can we help you?"

"Yes, hello. Three cheese slices for me and two for my son." Dad looks at me, then around at the place.

The cashier eyes me for some reason—maybe to make sure I'm okay.

I nod.

He moves his hands to the register and starts ringing us up. "Name?"

"Jake." Dad checks out the people sitting down and barely looks at the guy, but then that's how he does with most cashiers right before he tells me: You see, Son, you don't wanna be earning minimum wage like these scumbags. You wanna make something of your life.

It's as if I can hear that ugliness coming out of his mouth right now, like it's the millionth time he's blabbed it at me.

"Come on, Son. Let's go sit at the stools."

"You like the stools, huh, Pop? Reminds me of us eating hot chili at the Kmart food counter and you crushing saltine crackers all over yours."

"How you doing now that your sister is living in California?" He looks out over the half wall to the mall's center, where people are walking around. He turns to me—his brown eyes sparkling.

"I don't like it. I miss her." I mean, what do you want me to say to that? Tears want to come, and I want to strangle you at the same time. I don't want to be sad, and I don't want you to be sad. I don't want to say anything about anything.

He puts his hand on my back and starts tearing.

Mine start to gush out. I cover my eyes and try not to gasp too loud. But I breathe fast, in waves, and quiet.

"Ya, that is not easy, man. I am sorry for that."

Another crying gush. My throat grabs. He holds me across my side, and I start to calm down.

"Jake! Jake!" The cashier looks for us.

Dad and I wipe our eyes and hop to get the slices.

They're almost too hot to hold.

He unscrews the top of the chili flake jar, pours a shitload in his hand, and dumps it all over his slices.

"Dad, isn't that gonna be too hot?"

"Hey, man, don't you worry. I like that shit hot, ha ha ha." He laughs loud and weird. He shoves the half-folded slice in his mouth and open-mouth chews.

"Dad, there's steam coming out of your mouth. It's too hot to eat."

He moves it around so fast that it doesn't have a chance to burn too much. Eesh! Sometimes it's wild that he does that crazy stuff. "You know, Son, I was thinking to tell you, since Orly has now moved to California and your mom is moving to her own house, if it's all right with you, I will stay with you half the time and her also—you know, fifty-fifty. Does that sound fair to you? How does that sound to you, Son?"

I look at him. "Fifty-fifty?"

"Yes, man—we still do all the things together, you and me. Just I will be with you because you are my family, and she also is. And regarding moving you to the master bedroom of 6142, you will be safe there, man. We have Howard in the front and another guy in the room next to you. No one will upset you, I promise. They know if they do some shit to bother you, I will beat their ass. And, of course, I will sleep there in the master with you half the time."

"You mean that guy in that small room next to the master that has the little mirror that says, 'A friend in weed is a friend indeed.' That guy's not gonna bother me?"

"Yes, man. That is no problem. He is harmless—just smokes some reefer once in a while, no big deal."

I don't say a word. So half the nights you'll be gone?

"Okay, good. You will see. It will be all right. Your mom, she will be happy, and also I will be able to be with you, which I need very much, of course. Everything will be good. Okay? You will see."

CHAPTER 29

MTV Friend

Sitting in this kitchen isn't the same as 6140. This one has good light but is still sad somehow. The sliding glass door in the living area that opens to the side yard does bring in a ton of light. I like that I can see the pine tree, its deep-grooved bark, and the sky. Still, something's missing. Maybe a lot is missing. Dad wasn't around this morning.

Rrring. Rrring. The bedroom phone! Pop. I run.

"Hello—uh, hello!"

"Hey, Son. It's me. Why you huffing and puffing?"

"Ran from the kitchen."

"Okay, yes. I just wanted to check on you and that everything is okay. You are awake and all is good?"

"Good. Everything's good."

"Good. Glad to hear everything is cool."

"Uh-huh." I go quiet. I don't want him to get upset and think I'm questioning him, but I want to know. Is it true that he said he was going to stay and that he left in the middle of the night? I don't want to make him upset or, even worse, sad; I want him to be happy all over, and all inside him. "Hey, um . . . I woke up in the morning and saw you weren't there. Did you have to go?"

"Oh, yes, I do apologize about that. I had to leave early and take care of some business—something came up."

Something came up? Wonder what it was. But sometimes you just lie, like to everybody, all day. What could've come up? Maybe you got nervous that you forgot something or forgot to do something. You do get nervous in the early morning, especially because of all that army stuff. Maybe you got nervous and just had to go out. "Sure, Pop. I'll see you later, okay?"

"Of course, man. Enjoy the Saturday, and I will see you later, no problem."

The backyard looks easy and calm. A warm breeze swooshes things back and forth. Even the blades of grass move a little. The sun makes square patches where the roof and trees don't block it. Perfect day for a walk.

I head through my hallway. Maybe I'll scout down 441 and check stuff out along there. Don't usually walk down there, but today seems good for it.

"Hey there, little buddy." Howard floats out of his room, genie-like. He lowers his gold-rimmed, square sunglasses, dips his head down, and shoots those super-green eyes up at me. "Mr. Yagoobi, the second. Whatcha doing about to speed outta this here house?"

The room brightens up. "Oh, hey. You just came out of nowhere."

"Hey, hey, hey, now. I was just stretchin' these here legs and I saw my little buddy coming down the hall. Whatcha doing? You look like you's going out somewhere a little fancy." He giggles to himself.

"Howard, you're crazy." I laugh. "I was just gonna go for a walk. Wanna come?"

"Already been out. Just came back, matter of fact. Got my cigs and my beer." His hand lifts the aluminum can I know and wiggles it side to side. "He he he."

"Yeah, yeah. Havin' you a party. I know."

"Ha ha ha. You know me good. Listen, Mr. Little Arash, do you really wanna go walkin' to God knows where you fixin' to go, or you wanna keep your good buddy company?"

"Hey, I'm skinny. But I'm not little."

"True, true, you are tall for your age, but you always been tall for your age. Mature as my grandaddy, that's for sure. But those bones—we gotta put some meat on those bones."

"Yeah, yeah."

"Also, I'm about to fix myself some goodies: piggies in a blanket and them beans I think you like."

"Oh no, not the beans! They're freakin' delicious! Are you really making them?"

"You hungry?"

"I can eat."

"Come then, and keep old Howie company, and we watch us some good MTV music videos too."

"Sure. By the way, I like your shirt." My head tilts sideways and my eyebrows pop up and down.

"Well of course you love this shirt, silly. I bought one for the both of us. Think of you every time I wear it."

"Me too." I smile and look down at my identical half-cut, belly-showing muscle shirt. We start laughing.

He sets his beer down on the floor inside his room, takes out a new cigarette pack, and starts whacking the top end against his palm, again and again, making that clacking sound I hear all the time in this place.

"Hey, why you whack those smokes against your palm like that?"

"You gotta whack the top of 'em hard on account of it packs the tobacco against the filter. Give you a better draw—you know, when you inhale. They smoke better."

"Huh."

"Where's that dad of yours, Heecup, anyway?" He looks at me goofy as he pulls the thin red ribbon around the pack that pulls off its plastic wrapping. He takes out a cigarette.

"Don't know where he is. He could be anywhere. You know he can't sit still."

"Well, you know that Heecup is wanderin' around somewhere. We never can predict where he's gonna be next, that's true. Or who he's gonna find on the streets to bring in and be a tenant." Howard giggles to himself. His dirty blond hair catches the light just right.

"You wanna come inside, little brother? We'll get to fixin' them piggies and beans in a jiff. We'll have us a good little day."

I stare at Howard as he turns and walks into his room. I so wish I had an older brother. "Sure." I know he's kinda buzzed from the beer, but still—maybe he's too nice to me sometimes.

He walks in front—his mid-thigh cargo shorts, cracked-on-the-outsides white sneakers, and tan arms all say: "I am Howard, and I am proud."

"How hungry are you?"

"Medium."

He looks to the side, trying to figure how hungry he is. He nods. "Let's head to the kitchen then."

We walk around into the kitchen right next to his room.

"Pull them two cans of beans out from the cupboard and get the little sausage-wrapped piggies from the fridge. Mmh, mmh—so delicious."

"I like those beans, Howard."

"I'm glad, little buddy. Me too. The smokey flavor and sweetness. Howard likes hisself some piggies and beans."

My eyes move to every item on the kitchen countertop that's out of place. I want to turn all the labels on every can and bottle forward and align them perfectly, even the empty and dirty ones. But there's gotta be just enough space between each so that when you take one to use and put it back, it doesn't mess the rest up. It's way better that way. But it's Howard's stuff mostly, and maybe better to leave it that way. Not sure how actually hungry I am.

He warms everything up, fixes me a plate, and hands it over: five pigs in their blankets, a big scoop of brown beans spreading themselves out steaming hot, and a slice of white toasted buttered bread, stiff and half off my plate. I hate limp bread.

I look up.

His eyes stay half-glazed, and his skin is a little pasty. Definitely almost drunk. But he's so nice.

"Come on, let's cruise over to the tube. MTV is fixin' to have some good videos on—I just know it in my bones. Pull you a chair right here next to Howard's throne, he he." He grabs his plate and beer.

"I'll sit on the floor. I like it better, Howard." I do, and I snug up right next to Howard's chair.

CHAPTER 30

The Link

Hi, it's Arash, the dude writing this story. Hello (big wave).

Do you remember our first chapter: Dad bringing his crazy into the middle of my science class, and he and I having to escape right then on account of Child Protective Services was coming to collect my ass if I didn't leave the state pronto?

Right.

That goes into our story right here.

Let's recap the fun:

I'm sitting in science class, and Dad comes in to tell my teacher that we gotta go—that I have to leave Florida for a good bit and that we have to take off right away. We bolt out of the parking lot only for him to tell me that things with Shelby got hot, that he was an ultra-asshole to her, and that she threatened to call Child Protective Services because he was leaving a minor (me) alone at night. She was pissed. Dad and I raced to the Army Navy Surplus, bought the biggest duffle we could find, made a mess out of the place, and raced to my room to shovel my whole life into it. Then, we neatly proceeded to a hole-in-the-wall Irish pub to hide out until my flight was due. I was going to California to stay with a mom I didn't see and didn't remember since I was five. Dad wasn't going to let CPS take me away from him—no how. Then, when things cooled down, I was to come back home, back to Florida, just like I wanted, just like Dad and I had agreed . . .

CHAPTER 31

Moving Dots

Escalator down, and I might as well be on a boat. I'm gonna puke. Who is this woman I was thrown across the country to live with? Orly, please save me. At least you're gonna be here. God, please help this to be okay and let me get back to my dad. I close my eyes for two seconds and then open them. I'm nearly down, and my guts are in my throat. As soon as I see the heads of the people waiting at the escalator bottom, I wanna run back up, get back in the plane, and go back to Florida. Orly's hand waves crazy in the crowd.

"Arash! Arash!" She's jumping up and down.

I wave back. Why is she screaming? She already saw me. I wave again. She keeps screaming. Where's that mom?

Orly starts plowing through the crowd, rushes at me, and squash-hugs the crap out of me.

Ah, I never thought I'd be so happy to see her.

She pulls me through the people behind her, stretches out her other arm, and pulls a lady toward us.

Oh, crap. My eyes freeze on Mom.

"Arash, this is your mom." Orly looks at me, but I don't look at her.

"*Maman.*" Orly looks at mom.

Mom half smiles at me.

It's like someone has a hand behind my back and my front and is squeezing the living crap out of me.

"Hi, Arash. I am your mom. I am Simin, your mom." Her accent is thick, and she's just standing there, staring at me.

I barely get out a quarter smile. I look at her crisp brown eyes. Her mascara has the teeny thick blobs Orly doesn't like, but her makeup is nice. Her sharp cheekbones, skin as white as Orly's, and light brown, wavy hair down to her shoulders all sit there, waiting for me to speak.

She tries smiling again but also tries to hide the chip on her front tooth. She lowers her head to me.

I want to close my eyes and fall asleep.

Orly grabs my hand and pulls me closer to her. "Give your mom a hug."

Mom opens her arms.

My arms won't go all the way around, and they won't hold her tight.

"Good. Okay. *Maman, beeyah bereem tooyeh macheen.*" Orly turns to me. "I just told her, 'Let's go to the car.'"

The trunk of their faded banana-yellow Nissan Sentra pops open, and Orly and I dump the duffel inside like a dead body. The clunking of the trunk closing tells me how old the car is and in what shape the suspension is. Orly pops her front seat forward. I slide into the back, get cozy, and rest my head against the small triangular glass window.

"I really like the color of this car. Did Mom recently get it?"

"Yeah, a few months ago, actually, after she got her driver's license."

"Cool. These are amazingly reliable cars. Good cars." I rest my head again.

Suddenly, my neck snaps forward.

"Don't worry, Arash. Mom just hit the stopping concrete thing, but she meant to go backward. Happens all the time." She looks back at me and smiles with her pretty, bright face.

For about twenty minutes, I switch between dozing and looking out the window.

"Okay, we're here. This way, Arash." Orly waves me out of the car. Boy, she sure is happy here.

We walk the wide set of steps up; it's like walking toward a dungeon, the way it goes black at the top. It's gotten dark already. Where'd the day go? Mom goes up the steps, one at a time: right leg first, then she pulls the left up slowly, and then the right again.

"Hey, Orly, something wrong with her leg?"

"Her knee—hurts to bend it. Stairs are hard. Walking is better, but still hurts."

I want to race up, hold her arm, and help. What happened to your leg? Why couldn't you come out of Tehran with us? Why did we leave you behind? I wanna ask her a million questions, and I can't even speak to her. I have to learn Farsi.

"This is the courtyard, and our apartment is the one on the left, number 108."

It's dark out, but the courtyard's dim lights help a little. Mom's spotted curtains cover the windows completely. Weird choice, but whatever.

Mom opens the door and turns the lights on, and suddenly, all the spots on the inside of the curtain start moving, and fast!

"Orly! What the fuck? Are those what I think they are?" I scream.

Orly walks in. "Don't bother with it. It's fine."

I peek my head in and around the door to look for myself. "Orly! Dude! There's a hundred cockroaches running on the fucking curtains. That's disgusting!" It's like they're crawling all over me and through my hair.

"They'll scatter with the light and hide, dude. Don't worry, they only come out at night."

"Hide? So they can sneak up on me when I'm sleeping! Are you crazy?"

I can't take my eyes off those freakers. Of course they come out at night and hide in the light. Everyone knows that. Gross!

"Come on, Arash. Come to the bedroom." Orly waves me over. We dart past and over a couple of crawly movers. A quick right, and I shut behind us the big, heavy bedroom door that drags so hard along the carpet that no roach can possibly squeeze underneath. "Don't worry, there are no roaches in here. You're safe. And by the morning they'll all leave the living room, so it'll be okay."

"Yeah, I don't think so! Wherever they go, they're gonna come back, so, no. And you know there's always the rebel roach that likes to come out when he's not supposed to. I hate roaches. Ew!"

Orly puts her hand on my shoulder. Her gentle brown eyes and long, beautiful curly hair say everything's gonna be okay. She pulls me in and hugs my bones.

I hug her tight.

"You sure there's no roaches in here?" I look at the floor's corners and edges.

"I'm sure."

"How do you know?"

"I've checked."

"I'm gonna check too."

She turns to put some folded clothes away into the dresser.

I look under the bed and at the wall corners and slide open the closet doors to make sure none are there.

"*Een chekar meekoneh*?" Mom says, sitting on the other side of the bed.

"Mom is asking what you're doing." Orly looks back at Mom. "*Dareh dombaleh soosk meegardeh*. I told her you're looking for bugs."

I nod and sit back on the bed's edge with Orly next to me.

She looks at me as if to say, "I told you there aren't any in here."

I shrug, and my eyes sneak back to hunting the floor.

"It's okay." Orly looks at me with a sweetness that makes my insides disappear.

I put my head on her shoulder and my arm around her waist. She's the best thing in the whole world.

"We're gonna make your bed right here." She stands in front of a spot on the floor, next to her side of the bed. She grabs some sheets and blankets from the closet and starts laying them down, nice and neat. "I'll be sleeping right above you. Don't worry." She touches my cheek.

My bed looks like a secret fort hidden and tucked away, and if she's right about the roaches, we're home free. I love forts. I lay down, get cozy, and snug the blankets just under my nose.

CHAPTER 32

Family Missing

Mom's smile is weird. Her eyes are waiting for me to do something, or say something.

I ain't sayin' nothin'.

She cuts some butter to put on her bread, and she's already eyeing the raspberry jelly.

Orly dips her knife into the cream cheese, spreading it on the lavash bread like she's holding a paintbrush, clean to the edges.

"Mom said she wants you to relax for a couple of days. Then it's the weekend, and she'll take you to school to sign up for everything first thing Monday."

I look up and back and forth at both of them, then pop my eyebrows at Sis. "Do I look like I wanna go to school? Like ever?"

Orly laughs. "Hey, if anyone gets it, it's me. You know how it is."

I deal with my own lavash and cream cheese situation but don't bother to spread so perfectly. "Nice not have to go to school, huh, Sis?"

"You know it." She winks. "I do have hours to finish at cosmetology school, you know."

"Can you pass the strawberry jam?"

"You like the strawberry too."

I nod.

My eyes catch Mom's.

"*Azash beporse agar khoobeh.*" Mom smiles a little fake.

"She wants me to ask if you're good."

I nod at them both and squeeze my lips together.

"*Areh maman khoobeh,*" Orly says to Mom. "I told her you're good."

Mom keeps staring at me, then away, then another stare.

"Orly, um, wanna go for a walk?"

She looks at Mom, who nods. "*Boroh bahash.*"

"She says, 'Go with him.' Somewhere specific you wanna go?"

"I don't know. Walk around. You wanna go somewhere?"

"I have the perfect place! Let's walk over to the doughnut place up the road—they have delicious everything. My favorite is the chocolate glaze! Oh my gosh, what do you like?"

"I don't know. Let's go and check it out. I'm gonna just go outside. I'll wait for you. Take your time." I open the door like it's a jailbreak.

"Okay. I'll be right there."

A broken pot, faded brown doors to the apartments all around, and cracked, white-painted concrete floors are supposed to be decoration. This place is a dump.

"Let's go." Orly suddenly appears like a bouncy, bright angel.

And she's gonna take me to doughnuts? Sweet!

"Mom live here long?"

"No. She got this place after I asked her to come get me out of Florida a few months back. You know she doesn't know anyone here, except her two sisters on Veteran Avenue. It's about five minutes down Santa Monica Boulevard."

"I didn't know. That's gotta be hard." I look down at the sidewalks and the high grass on its edges. Everything reminds me of Florida. "You like it here?"

"It's okay. I really like being with mom. You know, I couldn't stand it with Dad. It was getting beyond impossible."

"Yeah, it was really hard for you. I remember. You fought with him like cats and dogs—locking horns all the time. Wasn't great with Shelby either."

"How are you doing? Just being tossed on a plane suddenly and told you had to leave—that's just crazy." Orly rolls her eyes like she knows exactly the kind of crazy she's asking about.

"Dude, I don't even freakin' know. It is crazy. One minute I'm hanging out with my friends, at school, all is normal, and then—out of the clear blue sky—on a plane, and now with you." I turn to her and smile. "What happened?"

She puts an arm around me. "It is hard. It's all really hard. Kind of makes sense with Dad's crazy-ass life. But you know what, you'll always be my little bro." She squeezes me, rubs my head, and pushes me away.

We laugh and turn left into a strip mall before the corner. "Tony's Doughnuts," reads the sign in big blue letters on a white oval background.

"That it?"

"Yes! This is the place!" Orly rushes to the door. "I can't wait to show you all the amazing everything."

"Everything looks delicious. How about one of everything?"

"Ha ha, you're tellin' me."

"Oh, shoot, don't you do it, Sis. I said it, but you're actually going to do it—who are we kidding? You're going to get one of everything."

"Nah, don't worry, we'll share." She looks at me with those trouble-maker eyes.

"That's what you always say. I'm gonna end up eatin' all that stuff."

"Um, hello. Yes, may I have the maple glaze, chocolate—yes, that one, the regular glaze, the eclair, and, oh, also the strawberry one over there."

"Oh my gosh!"

"I'll just have a bite."

"You always have a bite—two if I'm lucky."

The man bags them and hands them over.

"Here, you start with the maple—I know you like that."

I plow the maple bar down in the next ten steps. Delicious.

We walk down Bundy Dr., heading back. "What's the deal with Mom? Can she understand, or is her English really that bad?"

"Her English is not good. She just came here straight and hasn't learned any. Don't worry, I'll translate for you guys until it gets better." She looks at me. "You know, she missed you a lot." Orly's eyes won't leave me.

I look at her. Then away.

"She was happy to have you come out—I mean, like crazy happy. Not so happy that she knows you're going back. We talked about it, and we decided that whatever you want to do is fine."

I look around at the trees. Everything just got sadder.

Orly rubs my back. "It's gonna be okay, Bro."

I just wanna get into my floor bed, close my eyes, pull the covers over my head, and never come out. Maybe the whole world will go away.

"Did you bring those cool moccasins you love?"

"Yes. I did, and I really want to wear them."

She smiles brighter at me. "I love the tan suede color, that they come almost to your knees, and the fringes at the tops."

CHAPTER 33

Love Surrender

"Arash, Arash. Pelease, pelease."

My eyes burst open to Mom's face on top of mine. "What's going on?" My head turns to the clock. "Shit!" 8:47 a.m. School started at 8:00. Mom sees me freak out at the time, goes quiet, and leaves. I jump up, shoot to the bathroom, brush my teeth, try to wet and tap down my curls so I don't look like a total freak, and I shoot to the living room to find Mom.

She's already standing there, hands me a folded pita with cream cheese smushed in the center, and head-motions to the door. Her purse is on her wrist and her car keys in her hand.

Mom drives like a nervous wreck and pulls up to school before I can swallow two bites.

My fingers smash into the door, trying to open it. I put one leg on the ground, and suddenly, I stop. Everything stops. I want to get out of the car, but I can't. It's like I'm calmly glued to the seat, and I can't rush into the main office to make up some excuse about why I'm late. My heart, racing a thousand miles an hour, goes to zero. Everything gets deathly quiet and weirdly peaceful. I slowly turn to Mom's face. It's like nothing I've seen before—soft and glowing—like light is floating from it, all around it, and pouring all over me and everywhere. I can sit here and watch her forever. She's the most beautiful thing I've ever seen. Everything inside me falls and lifts together. I don't know what to do. Slowly, my hand lifts itself and says bye.

She lifts hers to match me, with a half smile that could melt a mountain.

I walk out, close the car door, and walk toward school like all the time in the world is here.

My first two classes pass like a blur.

The chalkboard in history class looks like the most useless thing. I can't stop thinking about Mom in the car. What was that? It was like our chests were connected on their own and wouldn't let each other go. I was so close to her, like we were one.

"Psst! Hey, Arash," Javi whispers from behind me as he stretches his arm across from his desk and taps my shoulder. "Wanna have lunch today?"

"Sure," I whisper back. Doesn't he know that we've been sitting with each other the last few days? Of course we'll sit together at lunch.

The teacher is reading something out loud that I can't even hear, let alone understand. The bell finally rings. Thank goodness.

Javier and Miguel appear out of thin air next to me as we walk out.

"You were so late to second period. Everything cool?" Javi looks at Miguel, a little nervous, and then back at me as we cruise to the cafeteria.

"Yeah. Woke up super late. My mom had to wake me up, and we busted out."

"Hey, homes, you sure you okay?" Miguel asks. "You actin' kinda funny, like tired or something. You get in trouble? Smoking weed?"

Maybe he can see something's off with me, that a part of me is still with mom in the car. "Ha ha ha! You serious? No, dude. I haven't smoked anything. I wouldn't even know where to get that stuff or how to smoke it."

"I got you, man. You need some. My cousin knows a guy. I got your back." Miguel winks at Javi and whacks him on the shoulder.

"Oh, you guys are funny. I think I'm good."

We grab our lunch trays and sit together.

Javier looks behind him, leans across the lunch table, and in a low voice says, "So you know about weed?"

"Sure. I know about weed. The people my dad rents rooms to in Florida smoke it all the time. It's all over the place."

"You being straight, dude? No bullshit?" Miguel says, his eyes popping out of his head while he leans in front of Javi so he can look me over with his sharp eyes.

"Dude, serious. The stuff is all over. The first time I learned about it was when we went to collect rent one day—I think I was eight or nine. We went into this guy's room, who's now next to mine, and he had a little mirror on his dresser with a picture of a weed plant on it. I asked my dad."

CHAPTER 34

Where'd He Go?

"**H**ey, Pop. How are you?"

"Hey, Son. You know, good to hear your voice, man. How are you doing there with your mom and sister and all that?"

"It's okay. I mean, it's hard. She doesn't speak English. It's really not good at all. Orly has to translate everything."

"Yeah, man. You know, that can be hard. You are right. But listen, now—I just rented out 6142, the master bedroom where we were living not too long ago. So now, at the moment, I am living here in Lauderhill— you know, at Shelby's house. We are here, and I am building for you a very beautiful room. It's like a Florida room but much better. It's in the backyard, just a little away from the house, and you can come and go as you please. You know, it is very private, and also very nice. I am just done with the frame. Then we put the sheetrock, and we paint it very nice and professional for you. You know, like when we had to put the sheetrock after those fuckin' drunk tenants got in fights and punched holes through the wall and shit. Yes, we are building now."

"Um, all right." My eyes roll around my head a few times. I want to scream. I want to choke him. What the freak! He'll explode if I give him an answer anything other than nice. "So, does this mean I'll move straight in there when I get back? Like into whatever you're building?"

"Yes, of course. Most definitely, man. You move in here straight. You will be with me and Shelby, and we will be together. Don't you worry."

But that's exactly it—I am worried. A separate unit? Backyard? There's a weird million-mile distance between us.

"Arash! Are you still there? Can you hear me? Hello?"

"Uh-huh, I'm here. Anything else going on? Anything interesting?" Don't go back to talking about what you're building for me to live in. Just don't talk about it. I don't want to hear another word.

"Not too much, man. I'm gonna go now and collect rent in a few minutes from some of these usual criminals. This one motherfucker Steve, man—he better have my money today, or I'm gonna kick him the fuck out. I might have to beat his ass, too, if he starts shit. You know I like to create some commotion, ha ha ha, but he better not fuck with me!"

"Uh, okay. I'll let you go and take care of business."

"You okay, man? I hear some shit goin' on in your voice. What's up?"

"Nah. Nothin'. It's all right." But what if it all falls apart? I can't tell him that. He's already a disaster worrying about me, although he won't admit it. I can't add to that.

"Hmm, okay. I see you are busy now. Let me go take care of some things. We will talk again soon, and we will be together soon. Don't you worry about that. You take care of yourself, and also your sister. Be strong, Son. Do good in school. Okay, now, let's say goodbye, and we will talk later. I will call you soon."

"All right, Pop. Love you."

"I love you, my son."

I hang up and don't know what to say. I don't want to say anything to anybody, maybe ever. Maybe doing nothing ever again is better.

"Hey, little bro!" Orly comes around the corner and heads straight for me, eyes sparkling bright and whole body bouncy and fresh.

"Hey."

"You just talk to Dad?"

"You know I did."

"I know. How'd it go?"

"Eh, I don't know. Sometimes I get off the phone and it's worse than when we started. He said he's building me somewhere to live in their new house's backyard or something. I can't even fucking talk about it."

"Listen. He's crazy." She lifts her eyebrows and looks as calmly serious as I've ever seen her.

I stay staring at her. She's right. But I don't want her to be.

"He does get crazy. You know that." She puts a hand on my shoulder.

"Yeah." I sigh.

"Listen, forget all that now. Let's do something fun. I want to show you this TV show I'm in *love* with. Obsessed. It's called *Santa Barbara*. It's a soap opera, okay, but like the best one. Come on. Sit with me. We'll watch together. It'll be good."

CHAPTER 35

Teeny Question

Out the window, the birds are chirping, the air is quiet, and most people haven't gotten dressed for the day. The street, cars, and even the trees are quiet. Wonder if Mom and Orly will come out soon for breakfast and want all the usuals. Maybe one of them will be sad today, or maybe everything will be just fine.

"Hey, brother man!"

I smile through the window and turn to her. "Hey, Sis. Your hair looks wild, and nice, like every morning."

She gives me a squashy warm hug, and sleep is still with her.

"Mom will be out in a bit. She's washing up. Come help me take breakfast out."

"The usual?"

"You've only been here a little bit." She squeezes her eyes together like I can't possibly know what she's going to do, or if I do, that I shouldn't say I do.

I lift my eyebrows fast a few times, betting I do. "Butter, jam, cream cheese, halva, lavash warmed in the toaster on two for three minutes, and pita slightly warmed on the gas burner."

"Yeah, yeah. Smart-ass."

"Hi. *Salam*." Mom turns the living room corner to the kitchen. Her silk pajamas are nice, and she's brushed her hair as straight as the frizziness will let her. Her face is clean. She looks nice.

"Good morning," I say.

"*Salam, Maman*." Orly scoots to kiss her on the cheek, softly and lovingly. "By the way, Bro, *salam* means 'hello.'"

"Yeah, I think I got that." I look at her like she should know that I know.

She scrunches her nose at me.

Mom helps bring out breakfast and stands next to me while setting the table. My insides pitter-patter, and I'm getting lightheaded. I wanna get away, but I can't move.

"*Azash beporse agar chaiee meekhat?*" Mom looks at me with laser eyes that expect something from me. I don't know what. She's saying things I don't understand.

"She's asking if you want some tea." Orly sits and rests her exhausted face on her palms.

"Still not a morning person, huh, Sis?"

"Fuck you." She mumbles through her hands.

"I'm sorry, what was that?" I laugh.

She flips me off.

"*Een cheezah cheeyeh!*" Mom says in a bothered, loud voice while looking sharply at us both.

"*Heechee maman, faghad shookhee meekoneem.* I told her we're just joking."

"*Hah, basheh.*" Mom's eyes squint, telling us not to do it again.

"She said, 'It's fine.' Take the tea, Bro. It's good."

"Okay."

Mom stands up to do something else to our teas in the kitchen.

Orly lifts her head and stretches over the chair's back, and cracks and crunches come out of her.

"Well, good morning, sunshine." I smile, annoying her.

Mom puts my tea right in front of me, on top of the plastic protector that covers the whole table. She looks at me and somehow through my eyes. I don't know what to say. What kind of look is that? Her eyes flip away and toward Orly as she goes to sit.

"*Azash beporse agar seh hafteh deegeh dareh meereh?*"

"She's asking if you're leaving in three weeks."

I look at both of them. I don't wanna say anything. "Yes. Tell her I talked to Dad. It'll be the beginning of summer. Things are back to being better there."

"*Azash beporse, meekhat bereh?*"

"She's asking if you want to leave."

I look down, pinch my nose, and breathe out. My guts drop into my toes. I look up at Orly and down at the plastic cover in front of me. "Yeah. I'm gonna go back." I want to vomit.

Orly tells her.

Mom's trying to be happy. We stay quiet for a few seconds, not looking at each other. My chest ache-tingles, and I want it to stop. "Please tell her thank you for everything she's done."

"*Maman, meegeh khaylee mamnoon barayeh tamameh karah keh kardee.*"

I pull my chair out fast, dart to the bathroom, crank the faucet, and cry hard. I put my hands over my face.

CHAPTER 36

Bunker 1

I don't like this plane. I don't like any planes. And I wanna vomit at the smell of airports, so I hate those too.

"Excuse me, young man. Just checking in on you and wondering if you need anything?"

"Thank you. I'm good." I smile.

"I have on my roster here that you're flying alone today. Is that right?"

"Yes, that's correct. My father will be picking me up at the airport in Fort Lauderdale."

Her face is so warm and bright. "Well, that sounds wonderful. If you need anything, just press the call button there and we'll take care of you. My name is Anabelle, and I'm the stewardess assigned to you. I'll be available the whole flight." She smiles and stands straight.

"Okay, thank you." Wow, she's so nice. Ugh, I'm nauseous. "Close your eyes, Arash. Sleep a little."

* * *

"This is your captain speaking. We will now begin our descent into Fort Lauderdale International Airport."

My eyes peel open. Shoot—slept nearly the whole time? I look around. Yup, looks like we're landing. Thank goodness. I couldn't be more ready to get off this thing. Who invented sitting in something way up in the sky doing only what birds should be doing? Doesn't seem natural.

"Careful now, watch your step." The pilot and stewardesses watch and smile as we exit. "Thank you for coming."

Can't wait to see Dad. My eyes lift to the tunnel-like exit that pours out into the airport. I know Dad is going to be waiting for me in the line. I take a deep breath. It's like the sun just lowered itself inside me. Everything's warm and bright.

"Arash! Arash!" Dad waves his hands high in the air—his massive bundle of keys clinging and clanging with the foot-long loop of red cord waving back and forth. Who could miss this guy? I don't get too excited or react right away. I love to watch him happy. I'll wait a few seconds.

"Hey, Pop!" I wave and rush for him.

He wraps his arms around me.

"I missed you, Son." He takes my backpack and holds me close. He squeezes me into his side, and a chill runs up my back. "How was the plane ride?"

"It was good. Okay. At the end I got so freaking frustrated, I just wanted to get out of there."

"Ha ha, but okay now, man. Do not get too hot. You know that shit will pass. All of that is going to be okay. Good to see you. Mom is excited to see you, and I am happy that you see your beautiful room."

My stomach sinks between my legs.

"Okay, listen now, how did your mom and Orly take it when you left? You know, when you told them you were going to leave, and then at the end, when you actually did?"

"Uh. They were really sad. I think Orly was trying to hold back tears. She didn't want to fall apart and make everyone sad. And Mom was already pretty sad. She got super quiet. When I told them that I was leaving for sure, I had to run to the bathroom. I cried pretty hard, but I didn't want anyone to hear."

Dad nods his head as he thinks to himself. "Okay. I know that shit is hard. I do understand what you are saying. But now you are here. We have each other, man. Everything is all right." He squashes me again into him, and it's worth tripping a little to walk together.

The airport's sliding glass exit doors open to a whole new world of being home and free. We cross the street and into the death-hot Florida sun. The sky says it's not going to rain today. "Hey Pop, we going to Shelby's first?"

"Yes, man. We take you there, drop your stuff, and you can get acquainted." We jump in.

Suddenly I don't wanna talk, and I hope he won't ask any more questions. My arm creeps its way up and rests on the car door, elbow sticking out and chin resting on it snug. Thanks, Dad, for not talking.

Errrrr! My side smushes into the car door while the tires make that sound I love when he turns race-car fast.

"This is the street. Another two blocks and we're there."

I look around the neighborhood. Seems sad and quiet. "This Lauderhill?"

"Yup, Lauderhill. Just a few minutes from our old house and the Army Navy you like—we're very close to it."

"Yeah, I saw it."

Dad turns a quick right and stops on a dime in the driveway within inches of the new-looking wooden fence.

"Nice, Dad."

The right half of his mouth lifts like when he means, "I know that was good," but doesn't actually say it. He pops out and yanks Mr. Duffle from the back seat. "Come on, Son. I want you to say hello to your mother."

"Hey, Pop. Why is there a cage around that front door?"

"Heh, that's no cage, man. That's a chain-link fence. Number one for security—so nobody steals our shit, but also for storage. You see how nice and beautiful it is? I closed the top also so no one can jump and climb inside?"

"So the pile of junk there in the corner is storage?"

"Come now, man. Don't say that shit to your father." He opens the fence lock and then the house door. "Hey, Shelby! Come out here!" His freakishly loud voice blasts through the kitchen, down the hallway on the right, and somehow hits its target.

"Coming! I'll be right there."

Dad tosses our bags on the floor against the old oak kitchen cabinets right in front of us.

Footsteps from down the hall say someone's coming.

"Hello, hello." Shelby's voice calls out. It seems like years before we see her coming. "Hi, Arash. How are you?" Her massive New York accent hasn't changed a lick.

"Hi. I'm good."

"Go give your mother a hug." Dad nudges me into her.

Hate it when he does that. I move to her and give her a non-squeezy hug. She puts her arms around me non-squeezy too. She looks at me for a sec with her soft, brown eyes. "How was the flight? All good?" She looks at Dad.

"Flight was okay. Everything was cool. Happy to be on the ground." I look at her brown straight hair and roundish light cheeks; they look soft.

"Good to have you. Did you see your place?" She points through the dark living room and to its side door.

"Okay, yes. Now to the left, through the kitchen where your mother pointed, is the dining room table, and that door there at the end leads out to the backyard and into your room. To the right of where we are standing now—the kitchen—is the master and two more bedrooms. I will show you that later. Come, let's go first to your room."

"Ooh, this is a nice backyard. It's much bigger than 6140, Pop."

"Heh heh. Yes it is. I built the fuck out of that one, man. We needed the space. I had to shove all those fuckin' tenants in there." He turns and points to a white shack-looking thing in the middle of the backyard, just behind the fence we parked in front of.

Looks like a sad old thing. I'm gonna have to sleep in that jalopy?

He jogs in front, opens the main door, walks inside a bit, and sticks his head out of the sliding glass door further down on the same side. "Son, come check out this unit, man! Come!"

I walk in. "Smells like paint in here."

"Isn't it great?"

"What is it, like six by fourteen?"

"No man! It's eight by sixteen, ha ha. Look here, your bed is in front of the sliding glass door so you get nice light. Nightstand right next to it here." He points. "You have yourself a small little hallway, and I put a beautiful dresser drawers for you over there across the main door, when you walk in."

I smile so he sees me and looks around. "Thanks, Dad." He gives me a soft hug.

"Okay now, you come into the main house anytime you like. The side door to the living room will always be open for you. I'm going to go in to see what is keeping Shelby. If you need anything, don't hesitate, man. My house is your house."

CHAPTER 37

Crunchy Things

Chirp, chirp, chirp, chirp. Chirp, chirp, chirp. Chirp, chirp, chirp, chirp.
"So loud." It's like a million crickets in here. Pitch dark, and outside too. No streetlights like 6140. 11:03 p.m. Shelby must be sleeping. But Dad—he's either wide awake, dreaming up some plan to be a zillionaire, or plowing through an Entenmann's Cheese-Filled Coffee Cake. What's it like in the house and sleeping in there? Is it more cozy than here? Gotta be. I toss the blanket off—too freaking hot—and I pull the sheet to just under my nose. Wish I had Debrah's number. My eyes get heavy and close.

* * *

Thunk.

"Hmm." Whoosh, smash, crunch!

My eyes pop open with my hand slapped against my thigh. "What the freak?" I lift my hand with the slime of bug guts sticking to it. "No! Really?" I know before I turn the light on. The falling sound from the ceiling, me slapping it to crunch death against my thigh, and the disgust of it sticking to my hand. I cup it so it doesn't fall. Click. Lights on. "Gross!" Cockroach! "Ahhh!" I open the glass door and wrist flick it as far away as possible. Two more flicks, Arash—can't take any chances. I rub my hand on the grass to clean it. Grass is always good to clean your hand, for sure. Gotta get inside the house to wash this disgust off. I step outside. Freak, it's dark out here. I grab the side-door knob. Twist, click. Twist, twist—click, click. "Aah!" It's locked. Be quiet, Arash. They said it was going to be open in case I needed to come in and use the bathroom. "Ugh!" Maybe I can find the hose on the side of the house. But it's pitch freakin' dark. I stumble back to my room, look at my hand, and smell it. "Bleh!" Ten times worse than the worst-smelling black mold I've ever seen. I'm gonna puke. I need a sock! Put your hand in as deep as you can. Now lay on your side, Arash. Keep that hand on your thigh. And don't move all the night. You don't move, the sock doesn't come off, and no cockroach stank gets rubbed all over.

* * *

Sunlight blasts me awake. I pop up and inspect the sock. "Whew." Still in place!

I dart to the hose and rinse like a crazy man. I scrub in a jillion different directions on the grass for an extra clean. Need soap. I look up at the sky and stop. A beautiful blue. Even the occasional white cloud is powerful and slow.

Click, click. Squeeeak. The knob on the side door above me starts to turn. My eyes bug out. Someone is saving me right now! Dad slips his head through, and it bends to find me.

"Fuck you doing down there, man? You crazy or some shit? Whatcha doin' with that hose next to you? It's early and shit. Say something."

"Thank God it's you! Had to wash my hands. A roach fell on my leg in the middle of the night and I slapped it in my sleep. I went to come in the house, and the door was locked, so I wrapped it with a sock." I hold up my cockroach hand. "I just woke up and was squatting down to rinse when, thank God, you came out."

"What the fuck?" He looks me up and down. He sees my wet hands, and immediately, his tongue comes out in that wiggly, disgusted way, with gagging sounds.

He turns to the inside of the house. "Shelby! Get the fuck out here, man! What the fuck? Why you lock the door on Arash and he could not get into the house!" He turns back to me. "That shit is disgusting, man. You know I hate roaches and shit. Go get you cleaned up with soap. And don't talk no more about those fucking roaches."

I lower my head and walk in the house.

CHAPTER 38

Pizza Go

"Come on. We're taking the Supra." Dad slips into the striped blue cloth seats that hug our thighs and sides good.

I love this thing—totally a race car. I jump in, click in the dark blue seatbelt, sit straight, and everything is bright and happy. Dad's eyes check me from the side. He's happy too. He nods to himself and peels out backward into the street.

"Let's go for pizza." His eyebrows hop at me.

"Same place?"

"Uh-huh."

"Cool." I look ahead, out my window, and all over.

"It's good to have lunch together, right?" He looks at me again.

I nod, looking at him with a half smile. I look straight ahead, down

Highway 441 as far as I can see. That's a lot of cars. A lot of people.

We pull in, jump out, and walk together.

"Hello, gentlemen. How can I help you?"

I look at Dad.

"Hello. Yes, we will take five slices of plain cheese—three for me and two for my son. Make them hot, please—we do appreciate you." Dad looks at the guy in a happier way than usual, and at me too.

"I love it when it's hot, man, ha ha." He puts his arm around me, and we walk to the stools.

He keeps looking at me—on and off—intense and kind. This is weird. Why is he acting like this? I stare at the chili flakes, parmesan, and napkin holder on the table. Something's up.

"Hey, Son, I wanna ask you—" He looks around and down, squeezes his lips, and looks at me deep and intense.

Oh jeez, please, God. Not the doctor talk again. I know, I know, be a doctor or lawyer—don't flip burgers, blah blah blah—just not the speech. I can't take the speech he's blabbed a million times and secretly promised to himself to blab a million more. Suddenly, he looks heavy and serious.

"I want to ask you, man. And I want you to be honest with me. Are you doing okay? You don't seem yourself—hangin' around here and there. You seem bored, and that is not like you, man. Anytime you like, you go here and there, walk around by yourself—find shit to do. You know— keep yourself busy and happy. You are good at that. But now, that is not happening. I know you don't have your friends at the moment—it is summertime. And also the living situation is new and different. I understand that. But it seems to me you are a little down."

I hate it when he knows everything. Why does he know everything? I look around for a sec. "I don't know. Everything is so different. I miss my friends. I miss Debrah. I kind of miss school and everyone there. And . . . well, living in the side room—thank you for building it and all— it's just so different. I walk into the main house, and I don't know what to do, who to talk to, or where to go. It doesn't seem like I belong there. I just walk back to my room." I look down, but he can see my eyes. If he touches me, I'll start crying. He moves his hand to my cheek and wipes the corner of my eye.

He starts sniffling too.

I can't look.

He pulls our stools together and my shoulder into his chest. He puts his arms around me and keeps them there. He really seems here and like he's listening. "Okay, we're gonna get you out of there. You and me—it'll be you and me, and we move back to 6142 together. I'll make the master bedroom ready. We'll be all right."

CHAPTER 39

Together Again

"**H**ere we are. Is it good? Do you like it?"

Same big master bedroom. Same bed, same dresser, same everything. "Hey, Pop, who was the guy who was in here?"

"Some guy I found selling newspapers. You know, they make a certain amount of money every week—usually it's quarters. They gotta stand in the hot sun, in the intersections, selling papers and collecting change. Then, you know how it goes, I gotta collect that shit from them before they blow it on cigarettes and beer and shit."

"I know. And you moved him to 6140?"

"Yes, it was a smaller room there, and it became available. We got lucky, man."

I nod at the pretty day outside.

"Thump."

Dad tosses the duffle on the bed.

"Dad, can we throw that thing in the garbage?"

"Why would we do that, man? It is a beautiful and perfect bag. Also, it's very strong."

"I hate looking at it."

He suddenly looks up and sees my eyes. "Consider it gone."

"Hey, you two. Welcome back. Movin' in, I see."

"Hey, Howard!" I run over, give him a ginormous hug, and hold tight.

"Hey, Howard, man. Good to see you. What's up?" Dad gives Howard the stink eye once-over. "Yes, you see, in the meantime, we are moving back in. Arash was not happy at the other house, though I did make him a beautiful little cabin in the backyard, and I did not like that he was unhappy. We want our man to be happy."

"Good to see you, Arash. Hey, Jake. Yes sir, that is a great point—Arash here deserves to be happy. I totally agree." Howard leans against the doorway like he's been standing there his whole life. He stares at me, suddenly smiles, and bounces his body off the wall.

"Drinking at 11:30 a.m., Howard?" I stare at the brown paper bag that covers the beer can in his hand until he sees me. I pop my eyebrows at him.

"Aw, this? I ain't drank but nearly half. It ain't nothin', little buddy. Just a little liquid good life." He smiles with his eyes almost closed.

Dad keeps stretching his arm deep for the last of the clothes.

"Whatcha got in there, Jake—the whole city of Fort Lauderdale?"

All eyes go to the duffle.

"Howard, that is the biggest one they had at the Army Navy." I look at him, laughing.

"I bet it was."

"Alright, let's wrap up, Son."

"Okay, you two. I'll see you later there, little buddy. You guys have yourselves a nice day."

"Howard—see you, bud!" I shoot my hand in the air and wave.

Dad looks at me, making sure to get my attention before Howard's even left the doorway. "How you like bein' back? Comfortable? Better?" He sparkles those eyes at me.

I look at the backyard, then at him. "It's really good."

He nods his head and goes to fold some clothes, but sits on the bed instead. "Again, I am sorry that you were lonely, man—like an outsider and shit. And you know I do not want you to experience that. Fuck that. We will be here together." His eyes are strong. They look throughout the room. "Now, I do wanna tell you that some nights I will go there, to sleep at the other house, like we talked about before, with Shelby. She is my wife, and I have a duty to her also. I have a duty to you also, and so I will see you one night and her one night—fifty-fifty, so it's fair to everybody."

I nod, but can barely look at him.

He stands up, puts his hand on my shoulder, and strolls out, not knowing exactly where he's going.

I sit on the bed and look out at the sunny yard.

CHAPTER 40

Miracle Numbers

"Hey, Arash."

"Hey, Charles."

"Hi, Arash." Angela passes by. Her eyes peek at me, her arms hold her notebook tight, she tucks her chin down, and the corner of her lips lift up.

I like that she's shy around me.

"Hey, Bro, nice to see you back." Samuel high-fives me.

The first bell hasn't even rung, and everyone's happy to see me back.

"Araaash! Duude!" He puts his hand out and cocks his head back to the side.

"Rico!"

We high-five and big hug.

"Dude, what the freak is going on? So nice to see you. Man, I didn't like it without you—no one to talk to in the mornings in front of school, no math buddy. How have you been?"

"Dude, it's okay. Like crazy. When I had to take off—what a mess. I wanna tell you about it. Lunch later?"

"Definitely, dude. You buying lunch today?"

"Of course. You bring yours?"

"You know it."

"Ha ha, Rico, I'll catch you." Another high-five snap! I love the calm around him, and that's around us when we hang out.

The day passes like a blur. Time, clocks, teachers' faces. I love the first day. And I hate it too: all the have-tos, homework, be on time, do this, don't do that. Lunch is my favorite though—nobody's on your ass, on your back, or telling you anything. You get to be free and have fun with your friends. Definitely, lunch is the best.

"Metal Shop, Room 162," reads my class slip. Hmm, where is that? Across from my old science room, I think. Can't wait! I've been looking forward to this bad boy since last year. Finally, I got it.

"Room 162," the door reads. Yup, lucky guess, right in front of science and across the outdoor concrete squares with the grass between them. The room looks okay enough: concrete floors, cool machines all over, but no teacher in site. Only a few kids I don't know are here. I spot a chair in the middle that looks good and slip my backpack down. The clock says I'm seven minutes early. That they let you out of classes early the first few days so you can find your next one is absolutely heaven. Rushing sucks.

Suddenly, from behind, a hand comes over my left shoulder. Oh no, I hope it's not that guy I pissed off before I left. Dude, I was not trying to take your girl, I promise. She kept waiting by my locker every day for days.

"Hi, Arash."

I know that voice! I look at my shoulder. I know those hands! And, oh my God, those slim, beautiful fingers too! I'm going to die right now.

My eyes look up to the prettiest thing I've ever seen. Those lips, with the perfect amount of gloss, and that wavy red hair that hasn't left me alone all summer. My heart jumps out of my body to somewhere far away I don't care about. "Hi, Debrah." My eyes fly outside my head, and I can't get them back. "What's up?" Don't screw this up, Arash.

"Someone told me I'd find you here."

"Really? In Shop?"

"Yes, I have my spies working for me." She smiles, glows all over, and touches her chin to her shoulder in a way that could kill ten thousand men.

"Uh ... what do you have now?"

"English."

"English, huh?" Holy crap. I'm so nervous. What if I don't say the right thing and she takes off? I hope she stays.

"I was thinking, what are you doing this weekend?"

"This weekend?" I haven't even thought about tomorrow. "Nothing. Not much." I shake my head.

"Good. 'Cause I thought we'd catch a movie."

A movie! Holy crap! What! No! What? She wants to go out with me? Can't be. "Um, yeah, that sounds cool." Good job, Arash, play it smooth.

"Awesome." She beams that smile that could crack a mountain. And I'm the mountain.

She tilts her head, letting all that gorgeous hair fall to one side. She takes her pen to the inside of my forearm: "(954) 469-6 ..." She blinks and looks right into my eyes. "We can meet at the movies at seven. Call me, and we'll talk." She doesn't take her eyes off me. Instead, they go deeper into mine. She tilts her head again, and I'm about to fall over.

CHAPTER 41

Van Gogh One

The front door opens as smooth as can be. I stop. Dad is sitting right in front of me, in the middle of the living room, more peaceful than I've ever seen him. He's super focused. His hand and the paintbrush in it move like one as he adds to the man's jawline, carefully and thoughtfully. With every brushstroke he lays down—he's moving, but he's still. The house is so quiet, you could hear a pin drop. My shoulders drop and I take a deep breath. He heard me come in, but he didn't move; he didn't get nervous. Just the opposite: he stayed painting, as if everything else in the world didn't matter and finishing was important. Perfectly fine with me.

"Hi, Son. Come in." He pulls his painting hand off, leans his head back, and tilts it, making sure the man's face on the canvas is coming along right. Satisfied, he turns and looks at me over his black-rimmed reading glasses. "Hey, how you doin'?" His eyes are warm and gentle and wrap all over me.

I just want to stand here and not move. "What are you up to?"

"Come. Come closer. I want to show you."

I stand next to him.

"You recognize this?" He points to the painting on the floor, leaning against the wall.

"It's the old wise man in a robe and turban, smoking a pipe—the one we had hanging in our apartment back home. Yes. I remember it."

His face lights up. "How do you think my copy is going?" He looks it over.

I check out the half-painted pipe man's face: white beard, a long pipe at his mouth, white turban and robe, and dark, tan skin with wrinkles so real, they could talk to me. "You know, Pop, he's starting to come to life."

"Yes, man! Thank you. Yes! That is exactly correct." His eyes dive into the painting again. "Look how his skin is so dark from being in the sun many hours. He's the old Iraqi men in the bazaars that would sit all day, sometimes in the direct sun, selling their rugs, lamps, and other things they sat next to. I remember their faces from when I was a kid. So beautiful they were." He sits back and looks at the original on the floor. His eyes pour out at it. He dips his brush and lays down more strokes. He looks at me with the gentlest eyes and back at the painting. "We brought that original one with us. It was painted by a master painter—one of the best. I made my father buy it for me when I was young. I kept it where I could see it always." He looks at it like he sees his whole world in it. "Unfortunately, I don't have another easel to put it on like it deserves, so I put it on the floor there, gentle and nice, in front of me, so I can learn from it."

I give him a long, warm smile.

"You doing okay?" he asks.

"Yeah, good. Good."

He goes back to work. It's like there's light shining from his face, his body, his everywhere, and it's moving through everything around us. Wow. "Ah." I take a deep breath. It's like someone lit a match inside me and the rest is warming up slowly. "I'll just stand here and watch."

"Of course, that's no problem." He stays with his pipe man.

A few moments pass like forever—long, slow, and peaceful, like strands of silk that catch in the wind and go on.

"Hey, Pop. You, uh, staying with me tonight, right?"

"Yes, tonight is your night." He dives into the left eyebrow, making tiny, delicate strokes, looks up at me, and smiles.

CHAPTER 42

Drip, Drip

"Wow, is it raining hard!"

"Yes, man. It was coming down all night. I couldn't sleep too good. You almost ready? We have to leave so you won't be late."

"Uh, almost." Slip my backpack on. Flip my rain jacket hoodie up. "We're gonna get soaked, just from the house to the car."

"Ain't that a bitch, man? That's Florida weather—you know it's fucked up. It's like what they say: 'If you don't like the weather in Florida, just wait a minute,' ha ha ha. That shit can change on a dime, that's for sure."

We stop just outside the door, still covered by the porch top.

Giant bullets come down from the dark sky's thick, heavy clouds.

"Let's go." He jumps to the car, unlocks his side, leans across, and unlocks mine.

I jump to the car too.

He shivers in his seat.

"What was that, about ten feet, and we're soaked?"

He doesn't answer.

We both shake the water off us.

He backs out slowly. It hasn't started to flood yet.

It gets quiet as he drives even slower. The windshield wipers go full blast but do nothing. We can't see but a few feet in front of us.

"Hey, uh, when I woke up in the morning, the sheets were wet on your side."

He doesn't answer.

I don't want to say more. "Did you go out last night?" Please say no. Please say something I'll believe. Please say anything other than you went to Shelby's.

"What did you say?" He pretends to look from side to side as if he's suddenly having a harder time seeing through the rain, although nothing's changed. "What was that?"

He heard me. He hears everything, this freaking guy, even when he's not listening. Dude, you can hear me down the hall from inside your room, half asleep. "The sheets—they were wet this morning."

"Oh, man, you know, I did go to get something from the car in the middle of the night, but then I thought—hey, you know, I wonder if Shelby is okay with the rain and all that, so I went to check on her. You know, no big deal."

He keeps looking harder than he needs to into the rain.

"You slept there?"

"I laid down with her for just a few minutes to make sure she is okay, and then I came back, man."

You fucking liar. I know you stayed there for hours. You're lying to me right now. You teach me how to spot a liar every day, all day, and you're doing it right now. My eyebrows scrunch, and everything goes Hulk tight inside me.

CHAPTER 43

My Gum What?

"Freak. Freak, freak!" Who said this is the way to meet up with a girl? Sit on a bench here in the movie theater waiting for her to show. This is crazy. I'm crazy, and also, I'm dying. Why am I so nervous? But I like her so much. I'm jumpy, and I could hop right off this bench and bounce all around this whole place. Thank goodness it's not busy—nobody sees me freaking out. Maybe I hide it pretty good. My eyes zip back and forth from the entrance to see if she's coming or if she magically arrived without me seeing. I wish I had a superpower where I'd be able to know exactly where she is and when she'd be here. That'd be pretty cool.

"Hi, Arash!"

The sweetest voice in the world speaks. I look to my left and across the room. There she is. Never has such tallness, skinniness, and loud gum chewing been so perfect. She's some floating angel, heaven-sent. "Hey." I wave my hand and stand up. Am I dressed okay? Is she gonna like me?

The closer she gets, the happier I get. Red lipstick, a little makeup, her hair pulled up from the sides and clipped up top—she looks great! "You look nice." I try not to stare at any one part too long.

"Thank you." Her nose wrinkles in the cutest way that is definitely going to make me die again. She puts her hands together, straightens her arms in front of her, and tilts her head. "Wanna go buy tickets?"

"Uh, yeah. Sure."

She smiles mega cute and hops a 180 toward the ticket dude. "Come on."

You damn right I'm coming. "Let's go."

"You want some gum?"

"Sure." Spearmint. I like spearmint. Bubblicious watermelon is the best, but this will definitely do.

We buy tickets, and she walks right next to me, her arm rubbing mine. "Ooh, there's our theater," she points.

We walk in. "Let's go over there." She beelines to an empty row of seats on the right, toward the back, and goes in first.

Dang, it's a big theater. Not a whole lot of people here.

"Have you seen this movie?"

"No, have you?" I can barely remember the title.

"Nuh-uh. But the trailer looks good. Do you like movies? See a lot?"

"Yeah." Like movies? Hell, I like being here with you. Who gives a crap about movies?

She gives me the brightest eyes, and the whole place lights up.

"There's a Margate Twin Cinema near my house. My friend Jimmy and I used to go there all the time. Super fun." I keep my eyes on hers. She doesn't let mine go.

She watches me and listens.

The movie starts. "*Can't Buy Me Love*," the screen reads. I can barely think straight. My head's racing a zillion miles an hour, and my heart's pumping right behind it; I think it might have jumped out of my body and onto that bench outside. Get a grip, Arash.

I reach over and hold her hand. Her long, gentle fingers slide between mine and fit tight. Our palms touch, and I snug mine into hers. She snugs me back. Our hands are a little clammy, but the absolute best thing in the entire world! I don't look at her, and she doesn't look at me, but I'm about to break I'm so happy. How could she not know? Oh God, all is so well that you can take me now if you want.

A few minutes pass, and it's like we've been sitting here for our whole lives. I don't even know what I'm watching.

Debrah leans toward me while her eyes stay straight ahead. "Spit out your gum."

What did you just say? Did you just say to spit out my gum? What? "What did you say?"

She leans in again. "Spit out your gum."

You did say that! Why did you say that? "Pfoo!" My gum goes flying away from both of us. She turns to me. Our eyes lock. Our hands pull us into each other, and our lips come next. Mine press into hers and hers into mine, and God still has not taken me. A light show starts exploding from both of us. I'm getting hot all over, and so are her lips, mouth, and tongue.

CHAPTER 44

Vroom! Friend

"**H**oward! Whatcha doing in the middle of the driveway?"

"Hey there, little mister. Just lighting me up one. Coming back from buying some cigs and hangin' out here in this Florida with my little buddy, Arash." He lights a match to the cigarette dangling from his lips. He curls the other hand around the match to keep the wind away. One deep, relaxed inhale, and out comes the smoke.

"You look good in that cutoff muscle tee."

"Why, thank you, sir." He looks up at the sky and stretches both arms out. "I do try to do my best, ha ha ha."

"Oh, jeez. Ha ha."

"You got any plans for this beautiful afternoon now that Heecup has gone to do whatever the heck he's doin' or he ain't doin'?"

"Nah. Just hangin'."

"Well, it's good to see you." He takes a "long draw" as he would call it. "How's that girl you went on a date with, the one at school? Debrah, I think you said her name was?"

"Oh my God, she's great. I'm great. We're great. We wanna go out again, definitely."

"Ah, that's real good, my little amigo. Young love is good love."

I love that you're saying that.

He looks around and takes another puff that puts him into heaven. "You wanna learn yourself to drive today?" He holds the cigarette between his index and middle fingers, his elbow at his side, and darts those green eyes at me.

"Serious?" My eyes open monster wide. "You're not serious? You're joking, right?"

"Serious as a heart attack." The sparkle in his eyes says he's being honest.

"What's my dad gonna say? He'll kill us!" My mind is going nuts.

"Kill? I don't think kill. He might be miffed at us—a wee pissed, but we'll cool his little butt. Your daddy is a troublemaker, you know—as long as we keep you safe, heck, he might even be proud of ya."

Oh my gosh! This might actually work. You're right about Dad, Howard. He might yell, but secretly, he's probably gonna love it. "All right then. Hell yes! Yes, I'm in! Let's do it."

"Good. Let's get you a phone book or two from inside the house. I'll get you a baseball cap. Then we go and practice in the parking lot up the street. And then, later on, if you do good, maybe we hit down 441 a bit."

"The Camaro?"

"American muscle, baby."

I dart inside and I grab the two thickest phone books in the kitchen I can find. I pop out. "This good, Howard?"

"Perfect. Let me get you that baseball cap." He strolls in and out of his room, easy and calm. "Now get in the car and put that phone book under your rear, and let's see if you's the right height."

I do.

"Now close the car door so I see you got the right look and that no cop is gonna pull us over. Last thing I need is that sheriff back at us on account that Jake the snake, your father, done gone and give us a name for ourselves on this here block."

I shrug.

"Ooh, you looking good! Now go on and put on that baseball cap and take my here purty aviation sunglasses and try 'em on." He passes them to me through the window. "Ooh! Now, that's the look we going for. Them cops will never know you thirteen. Shoot, they'd guess you about seventeen, eighteen, I reckon—you lookin' so distinguished and handsome and all, ha ha ha. You might even be more handsomer than me. Nah, you ain't. Ha ha ha."

"I love this!" I put both hands on the wheel and pretend to be a race-car driver. "Woo hoo!"

"Very good. Now scoot your little butt over so I can pull us to the parking lot, and then you go."

I hop into the passenger seat, *Dukes of Hazzard*, jump-over-the-center-console style, as if we're escaping from someone.

I look at him with sharp eyes as he turns the engine over. "Howard, you drank any beer?"

"No, no, my little buddy. That little swig ain't countin' on nobody nothin'. I'm just happy old me—you know—your buddy from Radford." He sports a big old goofy smile as he busts out his comb from his pocket and smooths his hair from the middle to one side, and then the other.

I squeeze my eyes and look him over carefully to make sure he's not lying. Nah, don't think he's drunk today.

We pull into the parking lot.

"Okay, now. You see, we ain't got no cars here and lots of space around. Don't go doing nothin' foolish now. I will be sitting right next to you. Let's switch. Now, I don't want that Heecup comin' after me for nothin', okay. So remember, slowly—press the gas very slowly at first and then the brake. The brake is the most important thing. Show me you're pressing the brake." Howard lowers his head from the passenger seat to check my foot. "Good. Great. Only your right foot works both the pedals cause this here is an automatic."

"Howard, I know. When my dad had his silver Toyota Celica, it was a stick, and he showed me how to use the clutch with the left foot and the gas and brake with the right. I used to love to sit in there and shift gears all day."

"Ooh, that's good. You got yourself a little head start, little buddy. Go on now, turn her over—that means leave her in park and turn the ignition key. Always keep that foot on the brake. Now, shift into drive, ease your foot off the brake, and let her roll natural—no accelerator."

"Oh, ho ho ho! Ho ho!"

"She's a rollin'." Howard rests his arm over the door and enjoys the warm sunshine. "Now keep your hands on the wheel, stay with her close, and press the gas, nice and slow. Mm-hmm, hear her hum nice and easy. If you get nervous, just tap the brake. In fact, do it now."

"Yes! We stopped! And I was going!"

"Good. Always brake slow, and if you're ever in trouble, brake fast."

"Got it."

"Good job using the same foot for the brake and the gas. Never use the left foot—I know you know, but it's a good reminder. With us, the left foot always rests on the side."

I nod. "Okay."

"Good, now let your foot off the brake and let her roll. Tap the gas, only this time steer a little left so we have room to turn around before the end of the lot." He watches me closely. "Good. You got you a knack for the steering?"

"Uh-huh." I stay laser-focused on the road in front of me.

"Okay, start turning right with your foot off the gas."

"This steering wheel is amazing to turn, Howard! The car really listens."

"Okay now, stop turning and keep your hands relaxed. Ease your grip on the wheel and she'll turn herself straight, automatic-like."

"It's turning by itself, Howard!" I take my hands off the steering wheel for a sec to show Howard how it's turning itself.

"Keep your hands on the wheel, just loose. Ha ha ha. That's right—she sets herself straight whenever you let off the wheel after a turn. Remember that."

"I can remember." I'm about to explode from happiness.

"Good. Now you got a runway ahead of ya—lots of space—just tap on the gas a little bit more than before and see what happens."

"Yes! Yes! It's going, Howard! It's going!"

From the corner of my eye, Howard draws another puff.

"That's a good job there, little Heecup, ha ha. You're keepin' them eyes sharp in front of ya. That's what Howard likes to see. Keep her steady now. Be prepared to hit the brake when I tell ya, but now a little more on the gas and hear her roar."

Rrummm! Rrummm!

"Yes! And, yes!" I practically fly backward through my seat. I hit the brake to slow down a little and then harder. We stop jerky. "Woo-hoo!"

"Well, not too bad if I say so myself." Howard looks at me with soft eyes. "Proud of you, Son. You're a natural."

"Can we go again?" My excitement stretches my face wider than I can imagine.

"Oh yes, let's practice some more. If you do good, next time maybe we go down 441 a little ways. I reckon you'll be ready for that."

CHAPTER 45

Steering Wheel

The sun warms my face and gently forces my eyes open. Look next to you, Arash. No. Don't. He's not here. And he hasn't been. He pretended to fall asleep with you, and probably not long after you dozed, he took off. And you know where he went. Why does he do that—say he's going to stay, promise, be so warm, and then break his word? It's like I'm a ghost: here but not here, but also far away. He said fifty-fifty, even with me and her. But it's not fifty-fifty. What is this, the third time? God knows how many times. And when I ask, some bologna excuse he'd never buy from the best liar he knows. How many times did I miss that he left and came back before I woke up? Something he'd do for sure. How many times will this happen again? Seconds pass like hours as I float into outer space.

"Get up, Arash," a whisper inside says. Nothing moves—not my legs, arms, or head. Just my eyes blink and blink. "Get up." Nothing. "Get. Up."

My eyes shake open, and I take a deep breath. Next to me, in the room, in the backyard—he really isn't here.

Why not go to the Sev? It'll be a nice walk—an easy Saturday. People in the neighborhood should be okay. None of that slow Sunday stuff.

I walk out to the front of the driveway and stand where I like, at the front of it, barefoot so the hot asphalt warms my feet. Things usually look great from here, but today, not so much. Dawn's old house, across the street and just to the right, is calm. No more playing tea like when you were seven, Arash. Gosh, I hope she's doing good. Those bright, sparkly blue eyes that looked at me so kindly when not many others would. And the way she'd pour us tea—like we'd been best friends forever.

The left sidewalk to the end of the street is clear, but it looks different than I've ever seen it. But the Sev will be good. The Sev's always good. Nice candy bars and a most excellent variety of bubblegum stand at attention on the top two rows. Let's see what's going on there today.

Halfway down the block, Mandy appears out of thin air and starts watering the lawn. Wow, that butt sticks out perfectly from those cut-off shorts. That unbuttoned sleeveless shirt, knotted just under her boobs, showing all that skin is always amazing. Normally, I'd stare, but I just don't care. And I don't wanna care. I wanna pass with no talking.

Just a little bit more, Arash, and by the time she turns around, you'll be gone. Go water the lawn away from me, girl. She's turning toward me. Shoot!

"Hey there, Arash." She narrows her eyes, tilts her head, chews her gum with her mouth half open, and puts a hand on her hip. "Whatcha doin', cutie?"

"Oh, hey, Mandy." I stop. "Heading over to the Sev. Whatcha up to?"

"Just taking care of the house a little. You know, somebody's got to." She smiles and shifts her weight to the other hip.

"Yeah."

"You doing okay, kid? You look a little . . . quiet." She chews her gum and looks at me as if she's trying to figure it all out.

I half smile, but nothing else moves. Any other day, I'd be so nervous just to talk to her, but today, zero nervous.

"How's your sis doing, and that dad of yours?" She tries to smile extra.

"They're okay. Orly is doing her thing, and Dad, well, you know Dad."

"Huh, ain't that the truth? Well, okay, hun. You take care of yourself now, you hear? You tell that sister of yours that if she ever needs anything, she knows where to find me."

I nod and get to walking. A deep breath comes. The sun starts burning into my back. Glad the Sev is close.

That orange-and-red number 7 logo and that green word Eleven never looked so good. I open the bell-sounding door and make it to my aisle. Bubblicious—all flavors. Tic Tacs—eh. 100 Grand bar—not interested. Snickers, Whatchamacallit—freak yes. York Peppermint Pattie—nuh-uh. And hmm, gummy bears—ooh, yes.

"Just the gummy bears and Whatchamacallit, kid?"

"Yup."

My butt thunks down on the warm concrete ledge outside. I dangle my legs off as I watch folks pull in and out of the parking spaces level with the street. Clouds come and go. Today, they're moving pretty fast—well, most of them. The air is nice. Trees too. And I like to watch all the people. My bag of gummy bears is almost out.

Eerrrr! Dad's '77 faded-brown Chrysler Cordoba turns the corner so fast that the whole thing leans on two wheels like a cartoon. Man, that suspension is shot.

"Hey, Son!" he screams as he sticks his head out his window before he's even parked. "What's up, Son?" He pulls his head back in, opens the door, and hops out. "What the fuck is going on?" He's excited and all over the place. He looks around in all different directions almost simultaneously, like an answer is coming from somewhere he doesn't see.

I won't answer until I have to.

"Look at this coincidence, man. I just came to pick up a few things here: some milk, bread, and a few things. How's everything with you?" He looks around again, and maybe if I delay answering, he'll forget about it, go do his thing, and leave me alone. Suddenly, he stops and looks right at me.

I squint with the sun in my eyes. "Yeah. Everything's cool."

He nods while looking me up and down; he's looking to see if he can trust me, his X-ray eyes seeing almost inside me. "Okay." He looks around again. "You gonna sit out here? No problem. I'll talk to you when I come out."

My eyes want to close. Suddenly, I'm super sleepy. I have no time. He's going to come out, and when he does, I'll need to be alert, fresh, and strong. I'll need to show him good things, positive things. I rest my forehead in my palm.

The Sev's door opens so fast that the bell hanging off it nearly flies off, dinging my ear to death.

"Hey, Dad," I say as he walks from behind.

"Hey, Son." Dad sits next to me. "Fuck you know it was me, man? Anybody could have been behind you? You psychic or some shit? Ha ha." He looks up at the sun, squints, puts his arm around me, squeezes me into him, and lets go. "Yes, man, this is beautiful, like this. I did not know you come here and sit like this. Almost like a meditation, man. Yes, it is beautiful now at the moment." He looks at me. "You do this sometimes?"

I pause. "It's nice here. Peaceful."

He squints at me and nods to himself.

He hops suddenly on the asphalt below and opens his car door. "Come, Son. Hop in."

I don't wanna go. I finally hop off.

I try to sit straight in my seat, but all I want to do is slump over, fall asleep, hang my arm and head over the car door, and wish he'd drive forever.

"Where you wanna go, man?" He suddenly rips the wrapper off the Hostess Chocolate Cupcake and shoves half of it in his mouth. He open-mouth mumbles, "You name it, I take you," as he barely chews the monster bite he took while squeezing the half-cupcake into the shifter and both together into drive.

"Home, I guess." My eyes float out the window to the hedges alongside the Sev's entrance and watch them blur as we leave.

In the three minutes to get home, it's like I'm watching the whole of *Forever*, all at once.

We stop. Good old 6140 and 6142 stuck to each other, sharing the grassy front yard. The house numbers on the side of the doors have nothing to say.

"How you doin', man? You okay?" His voice gets gentle as he looks my way. My eyes look at his and then out my window. My gut sinks through the car seat and the asphalt below. My legs go tingly and hollow.

"What happened last night?" I stay looking out, away from him.

"What do you mean?" I hear his shorts twist on the seat as he turns to face me.

I turn and look at him. His eyes stay half open and have that glaze on them, like before he says he's sorry. I turn and look straight ahead. "You weren't there when I woke up." A grabby heat rushes through my throat.

"What do you mean?"

"You said you were gonna stay, but I woke up at like seven fifteen, and you weren't there. And I know you weren't there for a while. You left after I fell asleep, didn't you?"

He stays silent.

"You said you wouldn't leave. You said it a lot. You promised. You know how important it was to me. Why did you do it?" Everything goes quiet, and I want to explode into a million pieces. I want to disappear but be right here, too, when he says the nothing that can make this right.

"Yes, you are right." His voice gets grabby, like before he cries in that way that he can't control.

I look over and tears are already coming. The corners of his mouth are pulling down.

He turns, sits straight, holds the steering wheel with both hands, and lowers his head as if to look between his knees. "I did leave, and I did leave early in the night. Man, I was wrong, and I was wrong the times I did it before. You did say not to, and I promised that I would not. I am so sorry, man."

My throat catches like speaking can never happen again. I look to the side, just barely away from him. Tears start to pour down, and I don't want to make a sound. I can't. "I can't share you anymore, Dad. It hurts too much." My chest crushes into itself from the center, straight through to my back. It's like I'm going to suffocate right here. At the same time, there's something deep and peaceful—like I don't have a choice. "I want to go to California and live with Mom and Orly," I say.

He bursts out crying.

Me too.

He stays put. His tears soak his cargo shorts.

I stay facing the windshield.

Tears pour from us both, like rivers that meet. Deep inhale gasping sounds come uncontrollably too.

Everything inside me—every part, every piece, cell, and thought, all say the same thing: I have to go. I know I do. And he knows it too. He won't fight me, not on this.

Conclusion

Congratulations on finishing the book! I'm so glad you did.

The clarity with which that singular decision to leave Florida was made is branded deep into my consciousness, to this day.

After leaving Florida, I never looked back, and never had a single regret. I just knew from that moment that it was what I needed to do, what I had to do: every cell, every bone, every part of my mind—everything, just knew.

Reuniting with Mom was as tumultuous as heck: time lost, trust lost, feelings of hurt for us both, and deep misunderstandings that made the distance between us wide. Later, after divine gifts and hard work, real magic grew back between us, and healing too.

Then, I went on to medical school and became a holistic doctor, and the call to write began.

Now, I am absolutely most proud of this book. I'm so excited about its existence and the privilege of sharing it with you!

Wouldn't you know it, inspiration has already sprung around a second memoir. Can you guess what it might be about?
I have felt a loving duty to expand the essence of *Freedom Boy*'s message: courses revealing its most vital truths and inspiration are now here!

Get the Courses: http://www.courses.freedomboybook.com

Buy the Book: http://www.freedomboybook.com

With big love,
Arash

Acknowledgments

Mom, thank you for everything you did, everything you were. I loved and love you so much, even when I didn't show it the best. May you open the underground dungeon you've locked yourself in—hopefully by the next two lifetimes, and get on with being your radiant self. Know that no one else has the key. You have all my love.

Pop, thank you for your hilariousness—it has been a big blessing to me. In your next life, may you be courageous enough not to turn your back on your artistry, or the world. May you live inside your beauty and your peace—it really was other-worldly to watch you paint.

Thank you, Esther, for the foundation of your support and your encouragement for me to keep going despite my flagellation and incessant fearfulness while trying to find the path. Your love is certainly powerful.

To Eliana, my eldest and eternally bright one—thank you for being excited about this project whenever I mentioned it to you or your friends, even though you didn't have a reason to or know why you were. You had the "knowing," as was obvious in your always light-up-the-room smile. Thank you, Rebecca, my middle, for holding the warmest, softest space in your deepest heart for me and this project. Your genuine interest in me and the progress of this book has been and is deeply touching. It continues to be my honor. To my youngest, Sarah, thank you for your power and might and for screaming in excitement at the big milestone of progress. I love it when you speak, and your maturity impresses me daily. It has been and is my privilege.

Thank you, Sis, for being the leader—I know it was insanely hard on you. I love you, and I'm rooting for you. Oh, and thanks, like super duper, for the Rumi book—changed my life.

To the rest of my family, I thank you deeply for your continued love, even though I erred sometimes. I love you guys.

Thank you, Kristin McTiernan for your editing and especially your story direction—I heard you and made the changes, and this book is tremendously better for it. Stacey Kopp—wow!—your meticulous proofreading polished things beautifully. Hat tip to you, my dear. Jason Arias, thank you for allowing the perfect cover to come through, for your patient direction and help, and for your artistry. It has meant a lot. Ming Lo, you made picture taking surprisingly fun, amigo.

Thank you, Navid—our lifetimes of friendship have been beautiful. Your effortless help is deeply appreciated.

Thank you to all my friends for your support and good wishes along the writing road.

Encompassing all creation and eternity in loving bliss, only a spec of which I have been graced to touch, thank you, God, Creator of all things, Mover of all action and thought, Supreme Director of all events, even if it appears to be bad or painful. I am learning to know that YOUR "bad" is always good. I deeply love you, and for some reason, exponentially more so when I'm noisily crying (don't ask—maybe fodder for a future book).

And to each soul on this planet that has ever come, is here, and ever will come, I love you, feel you, and am honored by your presence.

About the Author

Arash was born in Tehran.

He loves sharing his innermost feelings and experiences with his daughters, family, and friends. He loves studying the mystics and taking long walks with no destination. He loves cool cars in all sizes and varieties and has since he was young.

His labor of love is stringing words together. He is most proud of this book, *Freedom Boy*.

He connected to the magic of this world at seven years old and has been privileged to be led by its current.

He loves love itself and all wondrous things.

He's lost friends and family, yet gained many gifts.

He currently works as a spiritual advisor/guide in Los Angeles and sees clients one-on-one on a limited basis.

He loves writing and writes still.

www.ingramcontent.com/pod-product-compliance
Lightning Source LLC
Chambersburg PA
CBHW031317120626
46554CB00001BA/446